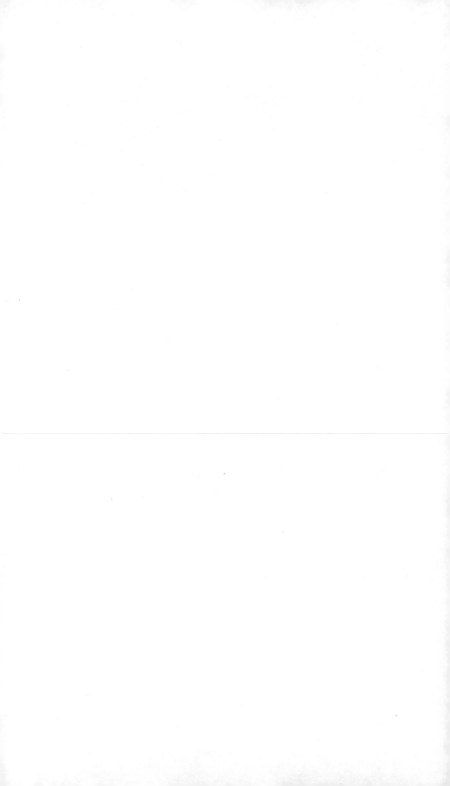

Modern **C**ultural
Theorists

Georg Lukács

The following titles are available in the Modern Cultural Theorists Series:

Georg Lukács

Stuart Sim

 **HARVESTER WHEATSHEAF**

New York   London   Toronto   Sydney   Tokyo   Singapore

First published 1994 by
Harvester Wheatsheaf
Campus 400, Maylands Avenue
Hemel Hempstead
Hertfordshire, HP2 7EZ
A division of
Simon & Schuster International Group

Typeset in 11 on 12pt Ehrhardt
by Dorwyn Ltd, Rowlands Castle, Hampshire

Printed and bound in Great Britain by
Biddles Ltd, Guildford and King's Lynn

British Library Cataloguing in Publication Data

A catalogue record for this book is available from
the British Library

ISBN 0–7450–1463–1

1 2 3 4 5   98 97 96 95 94

To Anne,
with gratitude

Contents

Acknowledgements

I would like to express my thanks to the School of Arts, Design and Communications at the University of Sunderland for providing me with sabbatical time to complete this project.

Thanks too go to my wife, Dr Helene Brandon, for invaluable support over the course of this project, not least with word-processing.

Abbreviated titles list

DR	*The Destruction of Reason*
ER	*Essays on Realism*
ETM	*Essays on Thomas Mann*
GA	*Goethe and his Age*
HCC	*History and Class Consciousness*
HN	*The Historical Novel*
HDMD	*The History of the Development of Modern Drama*
LSUT	*Lenin: A study on the unity of his thought*
MCR	*The Meaning of Contemporary Realism*
MHL	*Marxism and Human Liberation*
OSBH	*The Ontology of Social Being: Hegel*
OSBM	*The Ontology of Social Being: Marx*
PW	*Political Writings 1919–1929*
RL	*Record of a Life*
S	*Solzhenitsyn*
SA	*The Specificity of the Aesthetic*
SER	*Studies in European Realism*
SF	*Soul and Form*
TN	*The Theory of the Novel*
WC	*Writer and Critic*
YH	*The Young Hegel*

Chronology

1885	Born into a wealthy Jewish family in Budapest; father a bank director.
1904	Founder-member of the Thalia Theatre, Budapest.
1906	Doctorate at the University of Budapest; Doctorate at the University of Kolozsvar, Hungary.
1909	Continues studies at the University of Berlin.
1911	*Soul and Form; History of the Development of Modern Drama.*
1912	Continues studies at the University of Heidelberg, where he works as a Lecturer in Aesthetics.
1916	*The Theory of the Novel* (first complete edition not published until 1920).
1918	Joins Hungarian Communist Party (HCP).
1919	Serves as Deputy People's Commissar for Public Education in the Hungarian Soviet Republic (March–August). Flees to exile in Austria after the fall of the Republic.
1919–29	Living in Vienna; actively involved in the emigré HCP.
1921	First visit to Soviet Union; meets Lenin.
1923	*History and Class Consciousness.*

1924	*History and Class Consciousness* condemned at Comintern Congress in Moscow; *Lenin: A Study on the Unity of his Thought.*
1928–29	'Blum Theses', drops out of active politics when 'Theses' rejected by the HCP.
1929–31	In Moscow working at the Marx–Engels Institute.
1931–33	In Berlin; leading member of the League of Proletarian-Revolutionary Writers; contributes various essays to League's journal *Linkskurve* (published later in *Essays on Realism*).
1933–45	In Moscow working at the Philosophical Institute of the Moscow Academy of Sciences, and writing numerous essays which will appear in later collections such as *Essays on Realism*, *Studies in European Realism*, *Goethe and his Age* and *Writer and Critic*.
1937	*The Historical Novel.*
1938	Awarded doctorate in philosophy by Soviet Academy of Sciences for *The Young Hegel* (not published until 1948).
1941	Jailed briefly on suspicion of being a Trotskyist agent.
1945	Returns to Hungary and is appointed Professor of Aesthetics and Cultural Policy at the University of Budapest.
1947	*Goethe and his Age*; *Essays on Thomas Mann.*
1948	*The Young Hegel*; *Essays on Realism.*
1950	*Studies in European Realism.*
1954	*The Destruction of Reason.*
1956	Minister of Culture during the Hungarian Uprising; when government of Imre Nagy falls, is exiled to Romania.
1957	Returns from exile in Romania.
1958	*The Meaning of Contemporary Realism.*
1963	*The Specificity of the Aesthetic.*
1969	*Solzhenitsyn.*
1970	Awarded Goethe Prize; *Writer and Critic.*
1971	Dies Budapest: *The Ontology of Social Being* (Part I: *Hegel*, Part II: *Marx*) published posthumously (1976).

Preface

Assessing the work of a major Marxist cultural theorist such as Georg Lukács in the late twentieth century is a task fraught with difficulties when one considers the current reputation of Marxism itself. Marxism has been one of the most influential cultural and political theories of the twentieth century, but as the century draws to a close it gives every appearance of being in terminal decline. The relatively sudden collapse of the Soviet Empire and the effective disappearance of Marxism as a political force of any significance in Europe predictably enough has cast doubt on its credentials as a cultural theory, as have the spirited attacks on it from the postmodernist movement, for whom, in Jean-François Lyotard's now famous phrase, Marxism is a discredited and out-moded 'grand narrative'.[1] The grand narrative might appear to survive still in the East, where at the time of writing China still officially styles itself a Marxist state, but since the massacre in Tiananmen Square, even Chinese Marxism communicates the impression of living on borrowed time. Given such a background of crisis, any study of Marxist cultural theory will certainly be topical, although it also runs the risk of being, ultimately, an exercise in futility, for there is a very real question as to whether anything can now be saved from the apparent wreckage of Marxism as a cultural theory. Lukács becomes an interesting test case in this regard, given his eminence as a Marxist theorist on the one hand, and the range of his writings, on the other.

Lukács sets us special problems. Although recognised as one of the key figures in what has come to be known as 'Western Marxism',[2] he was associated for a large part of his life with the more doctrinaire, and now more discredited, Eastern European Marxist tradition. For much of the 1930s and 1940s Lukács was resident in Stalinist Russia, thereafter in Eastern bloc Hungary, and although he was later to be severely critical of the personality cult of Stalin, it is difficult to find him expressing any open dissent while Stalin was still alive. Lukács was also to the end of his career a staunch defender of 'realism' in aesthetic matters and a bitter critic of modernism (the defensive quality of the realist studies being a product of his '"conversion" to the earlier artistic style', Fredric Jameson argues).[3] Such luminaries of twentieth-century literature as James Joyce, Samuel Beckett and Bertolt Brecht will find themselves roundly denounced for ideological failings in the pages of Lukács' work. The commitment to realism can make Lukács sound very old-fashioned, and he was often so viewed by non-Soviet aestheticians during his lifetime, but with the advent of postmodernism and its radical problematisation of modernist aesthetics, Lukács' work is arguably more topical now than it has been for some time. The aim of this study is thus to position Lukács' theoretical writings in terms of recent debates in Marxism and postmodernism with a view to establishing his continuing importance as a theorist.

After consideration of the historical and cultural context in which Lukács lived and worked we shall turn to his contributions to Marxist philosophy, including the controversial *History and Class Consciousness*, *The Young Hegel* and *The Destruction of Reason*, as well as the late works on aesthetics and ontology; then in chapters 2–5 his major writings on literature and literary theory will be examined. In the latter case the trajectory is from the early works in the German idealist tradition (*Soul and Form* and *The Theory of the Novel*, for example) to the mature defence of realism, the commitment to which is maintained until the end of Lukács' career through a series of major studies (*The Historical Novel*, *Studies in European Realism*, *Goethe and his Age*, *Essays on Realism*, *The Meaning of Contemporary Realism*, *Essays on Thomas Mann*, and *Solzhenitsyn*). The Lukács–Brecht controversy, mirroring as it does a major split in Marxist aesthetics between realists and modernists, is the subject of chapter 6, and Lukács' political writings over the course of his long career are reviewed in chapter 7. The concluding chapters deal with Lukács' critical legacy – as seen, for example, in the work of such theorists as Lucien Goldmann and Fredric Jameson – the problems that Marxism has experienced in its encounter with postmodernist theory, and where this leaves Lukács' reputation. While it is in the nature of a study of this kind to concentrate on a theorist's major works, every effort is made to give a sense of the breadth and richness of the output of someone who was a very prolific writer indeed.

Ultimately, this study wants to insist that Lukács' theoretical concerns continue to have considerable relevance to today's debates, despite the radical change in the cultural climate in Europe since his death in 1971. For all that he remains a Marxist to the core, Lukács' works transcend the Marxist moment, as well as offering us a key as to why that moment failed to extend itself further than it did.

Historical and cultural context

Lukács' life was certainly an eventful one: philosopher, critic, literary theorist, politician, Communist Party activist and Marxist scholar, his career spanned two world wars, the collapse of several political empires, the establishment of Soviet communism, several revolutions, the rise and fall of Hitler and fascism, the dictatorship of Stalin, and more than two decades of Cold War. Variously resident in Hungary, Austria, Germany and Russia, Lukács was an active participant in many of these events and his writings cannot properly be understood unless viewed against a background of continuous socio-political crisis and unremitting ideological conflict. Such historical backgrounding is useful in the case of any writer, but crucial when it comes to Lukács. We are dealing here with a writer for whom political goals are pre-eminent over all others. Once converted to the communist cause, as he was by 1918, Lukács becomes a very single-minded figure, whose every thought and action is directed towards the prosecution of the class struggle and the achievement of the dictatorship of the proletariat. As often as not, these imperatives bring him into conflict with his fellow communists (he suffered exile and imprisonment at various points in his life), and Lukács' career provides a fascinating insight into the complexities of the power struggles within Marxism: power struggles which were ultimately to be instrumental in

Marxism's collapse as a political force in Western society. It is not the least of his virtues as a theorist that Lukács is so open to debate, so willing to subject Marxist theory to intense and permanent scrutiny. He was to insist throughout his life as a communist that Marxism was a method rather than a body of doctrine to be defended at all costs, and he was even willing, when necessary, to question the doctrinal pronouncements of such revered figures of Marxist history as Friedrich Engels.

Lukács was born into a comfortable, and socially and politically well-connected, upper-middle-class Jewish family in late nineteenth-century Budapest. He was precocious as a writer and started publishing as a critic while still in his teens. He also found local fame as a founding-member of the Thalia Theatre, whose aim was to introduce modern European drama (Ibsen and Strindberg, for example) into Hungarian life. Lukács' first substantial piece of work was a *History of the Development of Modern Drama*, in which Ibsen was lionised as the greatest playwright of his age. He also translated *The Wild Duck* for performance at the Thalia. From his teens, therefore, Lukács was part of a new wave of Hungarian culture, which embraced such figures as the poet Endre Ady and the composers Béla Bartók and Zoltán Kodály, whose concern was to challenge the bourgeois ideals of people such as Lukács' own family (with whom he had an uneasy relationship).[1] Although not a member of the Communist Party until 1918, Lukács voiced anti-bourgeois sentiments from a very early age and was soon in open revolt against his background, his communist conversion merely confirming a deep-rooted antipathy to his own social class.

The cultural milieu in which Lukács grew up was one undergoing a process of rapid change, in which old ideas were being subjected to vigorous challenge. The Austro-Hungarian Empire in the years leading up to the First World War was a cultural hothouse, witnessing the birth of modernism within the arts as well as the development of such ground-breaking disciplines as Freudian psychoanalysis. Lukács was later to reject the claims of modernism in favour of realism in the arts, but in his youth he is recognisably part of a movement to call into question the assumptions of bourgeois culture. Iconoclastic thinkers like Nietzsche were much in vogue among young intellectuals in turn-of-the-century Central Europe, and Lukács was no exception to the rule. In 1903 he is to be found praising Nietzsche and Ibsen as the greatest prophets of the modern age ('Nietzsche's kingdom is not of this world yet his ideal is the Superman, who stands as high among contemporary men as we stand above the apes');[2] while Nietzsche's influence lies behind *HDMD*'s Hellenocentric approach to its material. Lukács violently rejected Nietzsche's philosophy in later life, not surprisingly perhaps given Nietzsche's appropriation by the Nazi movement, but he is very much of his time in coming under its sway before the war. As Lukács' biographer Arpad Kadarkay has remarked of the conflict between the older and younger generation in early twentieth-century Hungarian life:

> While the fathers upheld national values, the sons signified their dissonance by devouring Kierkegaard, Nietzsche, Dostoevsky, Ibsen, Wilde, and Shaw. In one way or another, these writers are interrogative rather than affirmative. Above all, they delight in dissonance, and with near voluptuous indulgence shatter in order to rebuild values.[3]

Modernism was to push this process of interrogation, dissonance and shattering much further in post-war European culture, but for Lukács it was to culminate dramatically in the new system of values that communism introduced in the wake of the 1917 Russian Revolution.

Lukács dabbled in various intellectual movements in his early career – neo-Kantianism, phenomenology and hermeneutics, for example – as his studies took him around Europe (after attending the Universities of Budapest and Kolozsvar in Hungary, he spent some considerable time at the Universities of Heidelberg and Berlin in Germany, studying under such eminent scholars as Georg Simmel, Emil Lask and Max Weber). Undoubtedly though, the event that most affected him in this period, as with most of his generation, was the outbreak of the First World War. Lukács describes himself as being almost overwhelmed by despair at what the war portended for European culture:

> I arrived at more or less the following formulation: the Central Powers would probably defeat Russia; this might lead to the downfall of Tsarism; I had no objection to that. There was also some probability that the West would defeat Germany; if this led to the downfall of the Hohenzollerns and the Hapsburgs, I was once again in favour. But then the question arose: who was to save us from Western civilization?

(The prospect of final victory by the Germany of that time was to me nightmarish.)[4]

The war clearly propelled Lukács on an increasingly anti-bourgeois trajectory, and he noted with considerable disapproval the enthusiasm for the war among social-democratic parties across Europe. His major work of the time, *The Theory of the Novel* (written during 1914–15), breathes an air of extreme pessimism born of 'the age of absolute sinfulness' in which the author feels himself to be trapped (*TN*, p. 153). The pessimism was not to lift until Lukács came under the spell of Marxism towards the end of the war.

Once converted to the cause of communism, Lukács entered a very different world from the one of rarefied intellectual enquiry to which he had been accustomed for so many years. Events then moved very swiftly. Within a few months of joining the Hungarian Communist Party, whose members were initially more than a little suspicious of his motives (the party leader, Béla Kun, dismissing Lukács as a 'mad Heidelberg philosopher' unlikely to 'distribute the party paper at bridge heads and on street corners'),[5] Lukács was centrally involved in the establishment of the Hungarian Soviet Republic. Equally swiftly the Republic collapsed and, after a few heady months as political commissar for the Red Army's fifth division and Deputy People's Commissar for Public Education, Lukács found himself in political exile in Vienna, and a member of a fractious, faction-ridden, emigré party, which neither the Austrian nor the Soviet authorities knew what to do with. It was not to be until 1956 that Lukács was again to hold government office, this time as Minister for Culture in the equally ill-fated government of Imre Nagy during the Hungarian Uprising.

The political situation during the 1920s was volatile, and the many twists and turns of Lukács' career during these years bear eloquent witness to this fact. Some of his most important work emerges from this time: the *tour de force* of *History and Class Consciousness*, for example; so, equally, does the first of many attacks on him by the Soviet authorities (the vilification of *HCC* at the 1924 Comintern Congress in Moscow), and also the first of several notorious recantations or 'autocriticisms' of his own writing. The success of the Russian Revolution, together with the outbreak of revolutions in Hungary and Germany at the end of the war, even if these latter did prove to be abortive, saw the emergence of communism as an international force to be reckoned with. Marxist theory for the first time was confronted by the problem of political power, and this soon led to bitter dispute over the finer points of the theory and the nature of the relationship between theory and practice. Lukács became one of the central actors in this drama which, as Trotsky's experience was to reveal only too graphically, could have fatal consequences if one had the misfortune to end up on the wrong side of the Soviet authorities. Such an inventive and imaginative interpreter of Marxism as Lukács had to tread warily as dogmatism strengthened its grip on Soviet thinking, especially after the death of Lenin in 1924. The issues that theorists had to grapple with, then, were complex ones: the nature of the relationship between party and proletariat, the tactics required to create a revolutionary situation in a bourgeois state, the extent to which Marxism is a determinist theory, the role of the arts in a Marxist polity – these were some of the key topics on the agenda during the 1920s.

Lukács rapidly became a major voice in Marxist theoretical debate, indeed one of the few theorists of real stature to emerge after Lenin's death and Trotsky's eclipse. (Perhaps only Gramsci can be mentioned in the same breath from this era in Marxist history.) The contortions Lukács had to perform in his theorising indicate the volatility of the political situation within Marxism at this point, a volatility that was only to be resolved (if that is the right word) by the triumph of Stalinism and the effective suppression of dissent and debate among those within the Soviet orbit. Lukács was one of the first major casualties of the new dogmatism, and after the fuss created by his so-called 'Blum Theses' of 1928–9 (Blum being Lukács' code-name within the HCP), which recommended cooperation with bourgeois politicians in the context of the situation then obtaining in Hungary, he withdrew from active political life with one of his many recantations of his own work under his belt (his '"entry ticket" to the continuing struggle against fascism'[6] as he tried later to excuse it), not to return until the brief adventure of 1956.

Lukács' energies were soon to be absorbed in the struggle against fascism, and much of his writing in the 1930s and 1940s is designed to counter the cult of unreason which fascism fostered. Lukács was capable of finding unreason everywhere, in modern art and philosophy no less than in the rise of fascism, and his increasing commitment to realism in the arts is part of a wider commitment to combat what he called 'the destruction of reason' in Western culture. Aesthetics is a highly political area of activity to Lukács and after the collapse of his political career in 1929, he devoted a great deal of his time to the construction of a specifically Marxist aesthetic. Lukács' defence of realism has become somewhat notorious and it led him into conflict with such leading lights of the modernist movement as Bertolt Brecht, but his work on the subject represents a genuine attempt to create a sophisticated Marxist aesthetic independent of crude political considerations, and gains in stature when viewed against other conceptions of realism in the same period. This is when Stalin's cultural commissar, A. A. Zhdanov, was calling for an overtly didactic art and haranguing artists to become 'engineers of human souls':

> Comrade Stalin has called our writers engineers of human souls. What does this mean? What duties does the title confer upon you? In the first place, it means knowing life so as to be able to depict it truthfully in works of art, not to depict it in a dead, scholastic way, not simply as 'objective reality,' but to depict reality in its revolutionary development. In addition to this, the truthfulness and historical concreteness of the artistic portrayal should be combined with the ideological remoulding and education of the toiling people in the spirit of socialism. This method in *belles lettres* and literary criticism is what we call the method of socialist realism.[7]

Socialist realism is indebted to the work of the Russian aesthetician Georgi Plekhanov, who was firmly opposed to experimentalism in the arts, regarding it as a sign of social decadence. Cubism especially was censured, Plekhanov arguing that it was a form of 'art for art's sake', and thus part of a bourgeois ploy to keep art separate from politics. Plekhanov espoused a very mechanistic form of reflection theory in which art had an essentially passive role as a recorder of social trends; thus the determinist argument that 'Art, in periods of decadence, "*must*" itself be decadent. That is inevitable. And there would be no point in saying it is "wrong".'[8]

Lukács was resolutely opposed to such a mechanical approach to literary production as socialist realism recommended, and was a lifelong enemy of didacticism in the arts ('I am very liberal in such matters,' he remarked in a late interview. 'A good writer can be allowed almost anything'),[9] and of Plekhanovite determinism. In practice socialist realism inspired some very mediocre work, although it remained the official Soviet aesthetic for several decades, calling Marxist aesthetics into disrepute in the process. Lukács' defence of realism was an attempt both to come to terms with the art of the past from a Marxist perspective and to construct a model for present artistic practice; as such it is concerned to avoid the excesses of the modernists on the one hand, and the socialist realists on the other. For all its drawbacks (the almost total rejection of modernism, for example), Lukács' theory of literary realism is one of the few Marxist aesthetic theories which manages not to be either hopelessly elitist or crudely political in orientation.

Realism is an issue which has bedevilled Marxist aesthetics up to the present day, and Lukács is one of the central points of reference for the debate. The case for realism is that it renders art more accessible to the populace at large; the case against it that it is tainted by association with a bourgeois past and that it encourages stylistic conformity. Both sides agree that art is politically significant and they want to maximise its public impact; but the specifics of the aesthetic effect are so notoriously difficult to isolate that the debate remains inconclusive. Behind it lies a question that has vexed Marxist theorists over the years – that is, the relationship between aesthetic value and political value, and whether the former is simply to be subsumed under the latter, in which instance art becomes little more than a sophisticated – and if we turn to socialist realism *not* so sophisticated – form of propaganda. Lukács' contribution to the debate is to make a better case than most for art's special nature, but aesthetic value remains one of the most contentious topics in Marxism. When Terry Eagleton refers to 'the Marxist tradition's embarrassment over the question of aesthetic value',[10] he reminds us of just how uneasy the relationship between art and politics is within Marxism.

Another issue to bedevil Marxist theorists is the place of Stalinism in Marxist history, and here again Lukács is a central figure in the drama. Lukács was a notable critic of Stalinism after the dictator's death, giving us the memorable image of the phenomenon as a pyramid consisting of many little Stalins at the base and one big Stalin at the top, yet to all intents and purposes he appears to have done his best to accommodate himself to Stalinism between the 1930s and 1950s. Whatever he may have thought in private – and his claim in later life was that he was a bitter opponent of Stalin and his methods – Lukács kept his counsel at the time. There is evidence to suggest that he was more of a supporter of Stalin in this period than he afterwards claimed to be (even in the last year of his life he was capable of saying that 'it is sheer prejudice to imagine that everything Stalin did was wrong or anti-Marxist' (*RL*, p. 86)), and we have the interesting spectacle in his essay 'Tribune or Bureaucrat?' (1940) of Stalinist bureaucracy being attacked for being anti-socialist while Stalin himself is ostentatiously absolved of any blame for this development. Whether this is hypocrisy, irony or the selective blindness of the true believer it is hard to say, but it does indicate the scale of the problem that Stalin poses for Marxism.[11] Either he is to be seen as the logical outcome of a theory which puts too much faith in a centralised party apparatus, or as an individual aberration, in which case the theory's belief in historical process has to be temporarily suspended. Neither option is particularly attractive to Marxists, and it is fair to say that for all the efforts of the late Lukács among others, the Stalin phenomenon is never convincingly explained away and constitutes a powerful argument against Marxism's pretensions to human liberation.

The final phase of Lukács' career coincides with the Cold War and if he is anti-Stalinist in later life he is also virulently anti-American, remaining a committed communist despite the many vicissitudes that marked his relationship with the party throughout the 1950s and 1960s, when he had to suffer personal vilification, exile, neglect of his work and the death of many close friends and associates as supposed traitors to the communist cause. Lukács' belief in the rightness of Marxism never seems to waver (commentators such as George Lichtheim can be very harsh on him for just that reason),[12] but his history as a theorist illustrates Marxism's difficulty in turning theory into political practice. The Stalin issue aside, Lukács responded creatively and imaginatively to the challenge of transforming theory into praxis. And if he is one of the casualties of Marxism from the point of view of his enforced withdrawal from active politics in the wake of the rejection of the 'Blum Theses' (summoned to Moscow against his will, Lukács was made very aware of how little the party appreciated the really enquiring mind), when viewed against his immediate historical background, he is also one of the best advertisements for the virtues of dialectical thinking.

Lukács as a Marxist philosopher

Lukács is a major Marxist philosopher whose creative and imaginative reinterpretation of Marxism and its Hegelian sources, particularly in the influential works *History and Class Consciousness* and *The Young Hegel*, continues to demand respect, especially since it was so often undertaken in the teeth of opposition by the more dogmatic tendencies within Marxism. *HCC* remains one of the most appealing works in the Marxist philosophical canon, as its reappropriation by a later generation of revolutionary-minded activists in the 1960s attests. To such an audience the work's humanistic style of Marxism, full of the fervour of revolutionary Marxism at one of the high points in its history, spoke very clearly (Michael Lowy talks of the 'exemplary value' of the period 1917–23 for 1960s' activists).[1] It is one of the several ironies of Lukács' career that he himself had long since rejected the work by the time of its revived popularity. Thus we find him lamenting in the 1967 preface to a new edition of *HCC* that 'it is precisely those parts of the book that I regard as theoretically false that have been most influential. For this reason I see it as my duty on the occasion of a reprint after more than 40 years to pronounce upon the book's negative tendencies' (p. xxvii). The appeal fell on deaf ears, however, as *HCC* proceeded to become one of the most popular texts of the 1968 student uprising in Paris.[2] *HCC*'s humanist

Marxism was also influential within the Frankfurt School, with Theodor Adorno and Walter Benjamin both coming under its sway.[3]

The Young Hegel represents one of the most sustained attempts at working out Hegel's importance for the development of Marxist thought. Indeed, Hegel proves to be a pervasive influence throughout Lukács' philosophical career which in many ways can be considered a more or less permanent dialogue with Hegel. Lukács is also one of the first thinkers to argue for Lenin's credibility as a philosopher rather than just as a revolutionary tactician in *Lenin: A study on the unity of his thought*, a somewhat hagiographic but nevertheless still interesting response to Lenin's career immediately after his death. These works, with *The Destruction of Reason*, the posthumously published studies of Hegel and Marx in the incomplete *The Ontology of Social Being*, and the late work on aesthetics *The Specificity of the Aesthetic*, form the basis of this chapter's investigation of Lukács' career as a Marxist philosopher.

History and Class Consciousness

HCC proved to be a highly controversial work, not least in its outspoken criticism of Engels who, as one of the founders of Marxism, was rarely subjected to such treatment from within the Marxist movement, and its notoriety precipitated a series of recantations on Lukács' part. Lukács also deviated from Leninist orthodoxy on several points and was censured as a heretical thinker (guilty of 'old Hegelianism', 'revisionism' and 'ultra-leftism') by Zinoviev and Bukharin, two key figures in the early Soviet government, at the Comintern Congress of 1924. At the heart of *HCC* lies an almost messianic belief in the world-historical role of the proletariat, the class destined to liberate mankind from the clutches of capitalism through its developing consciousness, which is simultaneously the subject and the object of the dehumanising processes of the capitalist system. Proletarian consciousness is consciousness of reification, the process by which capitalism permeates all aspects of human existence and makes the social formation of capitalism appear a natural and unchangeable phenomenon. Lukács is thus providing, albeit in highly abstract form, an early formulation of the theory of hegemony.[4] *HCC* is a critique of the effect of reification on humanity and it advances proletarian class consciousness as the means by which it will be overcome. Proletarian revolution becomes for Lukács, as Lichtheim puts it, 'the key to the riddle of history'.[5] The overall conception is highly Hegelian. Although Lukács was later to dismiss his idea of the proletariat as the identical subject–object of history as a metaphysical construct only, it remains nevertheless a very dynamic one in the best revolutionary spirit of Marxism and it was to bring Lukács into dramatic collision with a Soviet political machine which was already well down the road towards dogmatism.

Just how undogmatic a thinker Lukács could be can be seen in his attacks on Engels. There is a refreshing sense of innocence about the way that he calls Engels' philosophical abilities into question, which was fast disappearing from Soviet Marxism: 'If on a number of occasions certain statements of Engels' are made the object of a polemical attack,' Lukács rather casually remarks in his original 1922 preface, 'this has been done, as every perceptive reader will observe, in the spirit of the system as a whole. On these particular points the author believes, rightly or wrongly, that he is defending orthodox Marxism against Engels himself' (p. xlii).[6] Perceptive readers within a Soviet Union in the grip of a Leninism heavily indebted to Engels proved few and far between, and there was also the small matter that *HCC* revealed Lukács' vision of Marxist orthodoxy to be highly *unorthodox*. But his self-defence is entirely justifiable: the arguments of Engels analysed here are philosophically very poor and hardly stand up to close scrutiny. In the course of a discussion on Kantian epistemology, Lukács takes issue with Engels' interpretation, and projected solution, to the 'thing-in-itself'. The relevant passage of Engels is quoted as follows:

> The most telling refutation of this as of all other philosophical crotchets is practice, namely, experiment and industry. If we are able to prove the correctness of our conception of a natural process by making it ourselves, bringing it into being out of its conditions and making it serve our own purposes into the bargain, then there is an end to the ungraspable Kantian 'thing-in-itself'. The chemical substances produced in the bodies of plants and animals remained such 'things-in-themselves' until organic chemistry began to produce them one after another, whereupon the 'thing-in-itself' became a thing for us, as, for instance, alizarin, the colouring matter of the madder,

> which we no longer trouble to grow in the madder roots in the field, but produce much more cheaply and simply from coal tar.   (pp. 131–2)

This is a quite drastic misreading of the Kantian thing-in-itself which is ungraspable *by definition*. The realm of the thing-in-itself, the 'noumenal', is precisely that which sense *cannot* penetrate. In Kant's own words:

> objects in themselves are quite unknown to us . . . what we call outer objects are nothing but mere representations of our sensibility, the form of which is space. The true correlate of sensibility, the thing in itself, is not known, and cannot be known, through these representations; and in experience no question is ever asked in regard to it.[7]

Things-in-themselves, therefore, are not *unknown* (because un-discovered, as in Engels' examples) but *unknowable*; they are not simply hidden away in the phenomenal world we inhabit, but exist in a totally different, noumenal, world beyond experience and sensibility. The thing-in-itself is ontologically incapable of becoming a 'thing-for-us', and as Lukács rightly points out, 'even the complete knowledge of all phenomena would be no more than knowledge of phenomena (as opposed to the things-in-themselves). . . . Moreover, even the complete knowledge of the phenomena could never overcome the *structural limits* of this knowledge' (p. 132).

These are unanswerable arguments, revealing a palpable failure on Engels' part to grasp the complexities of Kantian epistemology. This is a matter of some importance for Marxism, for Kantian idealism (where free will is a noumenal entity) needs to be overcome by Hegelian idealism in order to lay the groundwork for Marx's materialisation of the Hegelian dialectic and his promise that mankind can consciously, by the exercise of its own free will, make its own history. When thinkers such as Engels misunderstand the import of Kantian epistemology (the *unalterable* division of reality into phenomenal and noumenal sectors) then the idealist world-view cannot realistically be addressed.

Engels is also guilty in this passage, Lukács contends, of looking at science and industry in an unhistorical way; science and industry do not produce things 'for us' or 'for our purposes'; they produce things for capitalism, which remains the motive force behind their activities: 'Inasmuch as industry sets itself "objectives"

– it is in the decisive, i.e. historical, dialectical meaning of the word, only the object, not the subject of the natural laws governing society' (p. 133). Industry responds to the dictates of the capitalist system, in other words.

Engels comes out of this exchange rather badly, and it is clear that Lukács is less than reverent towards notions of orthodoxy in Marxism when these fail to meet the test of the dialectical method as he understands it. This can be seen in the book's opening essay 'What is Orthodox Marxism?', where, in a daring challenge to the dogmatists, Lukács asserts that Marxism's essence lies in its method rather than in any of its points of doctrine:

> Let us assume for the sake of argument that recent research has disproved once and for all every one of Marx's individual theses. Even if this were to be proved, every serious 'orthodox' Marxist would still be able to accept all such modern findings without reservation and hence dismiss all of Marx's theses *in toto* – without having to renounce his orthodoxy for a single moment. Orthodox Marxism, therefore, does not imply the uncritical acceptance of the results of Marx's investigations. It is not the 'belief' in this or that thesis, nor the exegesis of a 'sacred' book. On the contrary, orthodoxy refers exclusively to *method*. (p. 1)

This is heady stuff, even if it does come with the not inconsiderable qualification that the method can only be developed and expanded on the lines established by its original founders. Lukács is espousing a very open Marxism at a time when it was hardening into dogma in its 'home base' of the Soviet Union, and to his credit he retains something of that openness to the end of his long career, evincing a permanent dislike of sloganising propaganda where mindless quotation from the Marxist classics takes the place of dialectical argument. Thus we find him in 1963 berating the Chinese Communist Party (or 'Chinese-Stalinists' as they are witheringly called) for indulging in just such a tactic in the Sino-Soviet dispute, where 'the revolutionary catchphrases of overroutinized Chinese functionaries' serve to bring Marxism into international disrepute.[8] It is this firm belief in the critical role of method in Marxist thought that leads Lukács to treat Engels as fair game for attack: in such cases Lukács believes he is doing no more than defending Marxist method against its misapplication.

The tone of 'What is Orthodox Marxism?' is consistently anti-dogmatic and gives clear evidence of just how liberating Marxism could be for intellectual enquiry at this stage in its history, before it declined into stultifying bureaucracy: 'Marxist orthodoxy is no guardian of traditions,' Lukács insists, 'it is the eternally vigilant prophet proclaiming the relation between the tasks of the immediate present and the totality of the historical process' (p. 24). Again, this is heady stuff, assuming a moral rigour to the theory which sadly soon fell victim to the *realpolitik* of the period. Lukács shows Marxism's best face at such points – anti-traditionalist, anti-bureaucratic, global in its vision and local in its tactics.

Orthodox Marxism in Lukács' reading is a particularly dynamic theory (the dynamism of the dialectic is something that Lukács is always to emphasise, no matter what his subject of analysis). Here again, he runs up against the dogmatists and the growing belief, later to find its full expression in Stalinism, that there is a determinism about historical process that makes the proletarian revolution inevitable. Lukács is resolutely anti-determinist: the future has to be fought for by the class which is 'the key to the riddle of history' and it requires constant analysis of events by the party (acting on behalf of the proletariat) since the facts do not speak for themselves: 'A situation in which the "facts" speak out unmistakably for or against a definite course of action has never existed, and neither can nor will exist' (p. 23). Lukács is taking dialectics seriously as a method rather than as a set of prescriptions at such points; unfortunately for him Marxism is already well on its way to becoming just such a set of prescriptions and he will watch with dismay as it hardens into a bureaucracy – a phenomenon he regards as intrinsically anti-socialist. 'The objective forms of all social phenomena change constantly in the course of their ceaseless dialectical interactions with each other' (p. 13) he warns, and the Marxist theorist cannot afford any lapse into dogmatism or determinism. When this happens the theory loses touch with reality, and keeping reality in full view will be one of Lukács' lifetime preoccupations, whether he is working in the field of philosophy, literature or politics. There are few Marxist theorists of his generation with such a keen eye for disjunctions between theory and reality: one of his major objections to socialist realism is that it structures itself on just such a disjunction. Correct, that is, dispassionately conducted, dialectical analysis of reality is what Marxist method demands, and that will be a theme to recur throughout Lukács' writings, the need to identify clearly the underlying reality of events: 'For it is perfectly possible to describe the essentials of an historical event and yet be in the dark about the real nature of that event and of its function in the historical totality, i.e. without understanding it as part of a unified historical process' (p. 12). This difference between mere description and dialectically arrived at understanding is the key to Lukács' theory of literary realism where he will reiterate his demand for historical process to be made plainly visible.

The proletariat, in its role as the identical subject–object of history, has the capacity to grasp the underlying reality of capitalist existence, and its developing class consciousness is a classic example of dialectics in action: 'Class consciousness is the "ethics" of the proletariat, the unity of its theory and its practice, the point at which the economic necessity of its struggle for liberation changes dialectically into freedom' (p. 42). A dispassionate analysis of reality would reveal, however, that the proletariat is often a divided class, which requires the assistance of the party if it is ever to realise its world-historical objectives. What the proletariat faces is the hegemony of bourgeois ideology expressed through a variety of institutions, whose purpose is to deflect the proletariat from its world-historical role. The various institutions of the bourgeois state, the law, parliament, the education system, etc., present themselves as being above politics and history, but, viewed dialectically, recent history is in real terms the history of these institutions and of their operation in the interests of a bourgeois minority: 'so the need to deceive the other classes and to ensure that their class consciousness remains amorphous is inescapable for a bourgeois regime. (Consider here the theory of the state that stands "above" class antagonisms, or the notion of an "impartial" system of justice)' (p. 66). The amorphousness of class consciousness under capitalist ideology is what the dialectical method sets out to dispel. It is here that the party comes into the equation as the historical embodiment and incarnation in active form of proletarian class consciousness. Lukács' view of the party as a vanguard for the proletariat approximates to the Leninist position, although it should be said that he does not conceive of this role as a prelude to the establishment of a vast party bureaucracy, nor as any justification for it. For the Lukács of 1923, the party is there solely to assist the proletariat in recognising that it holds 'the key to the riddle of history'.

His essay 'Reification and the Consciousness of the Proletariat' sets out to explore how bourgeois hegemony seeks to keep proletarian consciousness divided and amorphous, but also simultaneously creates the conditions for its own overthrow by the combined agency of the proletariat and the party. If those conditions are created, then they still have to be translated into action, and the emphasis throughout this essay is on the need to foster the correct kind of dialectically aware consciousness, since Lukács believes that socio-political transformation will only work if it is the product of the proletariat's free action. Reification is seen to be the immediate reality of everyone living under capitalism, and it is based on Marx's analysis of commodities and the commodity-structure of the capitalist system. Marx held that commodities acquire a fetish-like character in capitalist society such that even human relations take on the nature of 'things': what Lukács wants to do is to follow up in more detail the ramifications of commodity fetishism and the commodity-structure for proletarian consciousness, so that it will become clear how their stranglehold on social development can be broken.

Commodity fetishism is seen to be a problem specific to mature capitalism. Although commodity exchange and commodity relations existed even in very primitive societies they never dominated those societies to the extent that they do under capitalism, where they come to form the basis for all human relations. In pre-capitalist societies the commodity form makes only an episodic appearance, but under capitalism the commodity form first becomes dominant and then is progressively hidden from view, as its character takes on greater and greater complexity, by what Lukács calls 'the veil of reification' (p. 86). The further into capitalist development we go the rarer it becomes to find anyone able to penetrate that veil of reification, so efficient does capitalism become in presenting its processes as the natural order of things, the 'human condition' as it were. 'A commodity is a mysterious thing', Marx pointed out,

> simply because in it the social character of men's labour appears to them as an objective character stamped upon the product of that labour; because the relation of the producers to the sum total of their own labour is presented to them as a social relation, existing

not between themselves, but between the products of their labour.   (quoted, p. 86)

The net result is that the individual's labour becomes something independent of her, assuming the form of a commodity she owns. The labour is reified, turned into a thing, and it is the commodity form that is directly responsible for this abstraction of human labour: at which point the veil of reification is firmly in place. Capitalist labour is measurable labour thus further entrenching the process of reification:

> time sheds its qualitative, variable, flowing nature; it freezes into an exactly delimited, quantifiable continuum filled with quantifiable 'things' (the reified, mechanically objectified 'performance' of the worker, wholly separated from his total human personality): in short, it becomes space . . . the personality can do no more than look on helplessly while its own existence is reduced to an isolated particle and fed into an alien system.   (p. 90)

The dehumanising tendency of the capitalist system is revealed in the way that it succeeds in transforming the human function of labour into a commodity existing in objective relationship to all other commodities on the open market.

Modern bureaucracy, with its machine-like character, remoteness from the 'things' to which its activity nominally pertains, and commitment to standardisation and formal procedures, indicates how effectively reification penetrates all areas of life under capitalism, altering consciousness as it does so. The modern capitalist state is an essentially bureaucratic organism whose various institutions are concerned not so much with the needs of human beings as with the demands of formal systems. Such institutions can only deal with human beings at the level of things, where social functions are reduced to their elements in order to ensure the smoother running of the system. Within the system all relations are the relations between things, which the reified consciousness sees as 'natural': the individual bureaucrat submits herself to the efficiency of the bureaucratic machine as the individual worker does to the production-line process. Human relations become a mere adjunct of the commodity form, and reification, in Lukács' emotive phrase, 'stamps its imprint upon the whole consciousness of man' (p. 100). As an example of just how deep an imprint it can make,

Lukács cites Kant's legalistic description of sexual relations: 'Sexual community is the reciprocal use made by one person of the sexual organs and faculties of another . . . marriage . . . is the union of two people of different sexes with a view to the mutual possession of each other's sexual attributes for the duration of their lives' (quoted, p. 100). The sexual relation, no less than any other kind of human relation, is to be reduced to the level of the commodity form. Kantian philosophy in general is the product of the reified structure of consciousness for Lukács, and the thing-in-itself bears eloquent witness to the fact – hence Lukács' dismay at Engels' inability to grasp what is really at stake in Kantian epistemology.

Reification would seem to herald the ultimate triumph of the capitalist system, but it also provides the basis for that system's downfall by its generation of a proletarian consciousness *aware* of the fact of reification. Proletarian workers are transformed into objects of the capitalist process of production by the fact that they must make an object of their labour-power and sell it to the system as a commodity on the open market. Objectifying oneself in this manner induces an awareness of being at once both subject and object, and thus of the process of reification that is at work; it can then be said of the worker that, 'Inasmuch as he is incapable in practice of raising himself above the role of object his consciousness is the *self-consciousness of the commodity*; or in other words it is the self-knowledge, the self-revelation of the capitalist society founded upon the production and exchange of commodities' (p. 168). When the proletarian comes to know himself as a commodity, that knowledge is practical knowledge; that is to say, it changes his view of the world and of the process in which he is involved. Labour's special role in the capitalist system, the commodity which above all provides the basis for profit, or surplus-value, is thus revealed to the worker, who comes to understand that underlying the commodity form, in each and every case, is a relation between people – and relations between people can always be changed, they do not have the same character as a natural law. In Hegelian terms of reference the worker's self-consciousness of being a commodity constitutes a shift from quantity to quality; it is the difference between being aware that one is being exploited by a system and being aware that the system depends precisely on one's exploitation (and others like one). The self-consciousness of the latter state is a higher stage of knowledge, which holds out the promise of qualitative change for the whole system. To become the identical subject–object of history is to attain the capability to overcome capitalism.

If the proletariat can be said to possess the capability to overcome capitalism and to substitute a more human society in its stead, that should not be understood to mean that the process is either inevitable or automatic. Reification needs to be constantly confronted and disrupted, its contradictions constantly brought to light, if the class struggle is to be successfully prosecuted. That leaves a significant role for the party as well as for the proletariat:

> Only when the consciousness of the proletariat is able to point out the road along which the dialectics of history is objectively impelled, but which it cannot travel unaided, will the consciousness of the proletariat awaken to a consciousness of the process, and only then will the proletariat become the identical subject-object of history whose praxis will change reality. (p. 197)

The proletariat has been given both the opportunity and the justification to effect changes in society, but its exposure to ever new forms of reification means that it may fail to take the step required. Neither will it work if it is forced to take this step: 'Any transformation', as Lukács points out in an explicit rejection of the determinist position, 'can only come about as the product of the – free – action of the proletariat itself' (p. 209). 'Free' in this case means deliberately chosen and deliberately planned, as Lukács steers a middle course between the determinists and such theorists as Rosa Luxembourg, whom he accuses of overestimating the spontaneous and elemental forces present in both the revolution and the proletariat itself. It is a characteristic of Lukács' critical method, as we shall see in the studies on realism, to seek such a middle course between extremes.

A critical role is thus allotted to the Communist Party in preparing the proletariat for its world-historical role. Its task is to act as the organised form of proletarian consciousness and to offer theoretical guidance to the masses, thus preventing them from lapsing into any spontaneous action, which can easily be suppressed by the bourgeois authorities. The emphasis is firmly on tactics and planning:

> it is dangerous for the revolution to overestimate the element of inevitability and to assume that the choice of any particular tactic might

unleash even a series of actions (to say nothing of determining the course of the revolution itself), and trigger off a chain reaction leading to even more distant goals by some ineluctable process. And it would be no less fatal to believe that the most successful action of the largest and best-organised Communist Party could do more than lead the proletariat correctly into battle in pursuit of a goal to which it itself aspires – if not with full awareness of the fact.   (p. 330)

The positive reading of such a passage would be to agree with Andrew Feenberg's contention that 'in Lukács the party does not have the proletariat at its disposal, but rather vice versa',[9] yet Lukács' vision of the party has been criticised as elitist, and problems are indeed opening up in his discussion of the relationship between party and proletariat in 'Towards a Methodology of the Problem of Organisation'. The party's ontological status is a problematical one, simultaneously the conscience of the proletariat but also having an autonomous existence apart from the proletariat. Phrases like 'The Communist Party is an *autonomous form* of proletarian class consciousness serving the interests of the revolution' (p. 330) merely lead us into a quagmire. Even given Lukács' insistence on the uneven development of proletarian consciousness – where some sections of the proletariat, for good socio-historical reasons, are far in advance of others – the spectre this arouses is the conclusion that 'the party knows best'. Under such circumstances the right action for the proletariat to take is the one that the party instructs it to, hardly meriting the description of 'free'. The humanism of Lukács' conception of the proletariat as the identical subject–object of history begins to dissolve when confronted by the vision of a party that 'is sometimes forced to adopt a stance opposed to that of the masses' and 'must show them the way by rejecting their immediate wishes' (p. 329). It all depends how this is interpreted of course, and Lukács does leave room for negotiation between party and proletariat (returning to the issue again and again throughout his political writings of the 1920s), but he seems nevertheless to be sanctioning a separation between party and proletariat which is unhealthy in the long run – as the Soviet experience was all too soon to demonstrate. As Arato and Brienes point out, for all Lukács' attacks on bureaucratic tendencies and calls for proletarian free action in *HCC*, 'the logic of his argument forced him to accept and justify a party that in fact satisfied few of the implicit requirements of his theory'.[10]

One might give Lukács the benefit of the doubt and suggest that his major concern is to ensure that the dialectical method retains its central place in the Marxist movement, and that there is no lapse into anarchic spontaneity on the one hand, or fatalistic determinism on the other. In the turbulent political climate of the early 1920s, it was only too easy to fall from dialectical grace. The generous reading of 'Towards a Methodology' would be to assume that what the party represented to Lukács was the purity of the dialectical method. Lukács' subsequent career does not provide conclusive proof one way or the other as to whether he conceived of the party in overtly repressive terms. True, he lived in Russia under Stalin and said nothing openly anti-Stalinist until after Stalin's death (though given Stalin's treatment of dissidents such an omission is probably forgivable), but his support for the Hungarian Uprising of 1956 surely deserves better than to be condemned by Lichtheim as 'evidence of personal inconsistency in that he half-heartedly sided with the rebels, thus repudiating the implications of his own elitism'.[11] Perhaps the elitism is more apparent than real, a product of the highly abstract, highly Hegelian, argument of *HCC* as a whole, rather than a justification of, or call for, a repressive form of party apparatus as such. It is one thing to make allowances for a theoretical argument, however, quite another to do so for the political practice of Soviet and Eastern bloc Communist Parties over a period of several decades. In the act of engaging with the issue of party and proletariat Lukács only succeeds in demonstrating how intractable it is; in Martin Jay's terms of reference, what Lukács discovers is 'the gap between empirical and imputed class consciousness'.[12] It proves to be an issue which Marxism never does satisfactorily resolve – the persistence of the gap undermining the claims of theorists from Lukács onwards to have found 'the key to the riddle of history'.

Lukács' 1967 preface is highly critical of *HCC*'s arguments, particularly of the Hegelian bias, which was to lead him into so much trouble with the Soviet authorities. The book's central thesis, that the proletariat is the identical subject–object of history – precisely the aspect that appealed most strongly to a later generation of socialist activists – is rejected as a metaphysical construct at variance with Lukács' subsequent determinedly realist approach to analysis. The critique of reification is said to be seriously flawed in so far as the terms 'reification' and 'alienation' are used synonymously throughout, although they cannot be considered socially or conceptually identical. Nevertheless, the book as a whole is not as radically different from Lukács' later work as he seeks to suggest. The Hegelian bias never completely disappears from his thinking – one can still see ample evidence of it in the realism studies – and the anti-bureaucratic sentiments, unworldly though they are, remain a feature of his work too. So does the insistence on the dynamic nature of the dialectic, and the desire to steer a middle course between the extremes of anarchic spontaneity and fatalistic determinism that a superficial reading of the dialectic can so easily lead one into. On one point at least the older Lukács finds himself still fully in agreement with the younger, and that is concerning the nature of Marxist orthodoxy. The emphasis on method at the expense of points of doctrine in 'What is Orthodox Marxism?' he describes as 'not only objectively correct but also capable of exerting a considerable influence even today when we are on the eve of a Marxist renaissance' (p. xxv). The sting in the tail, however, is that the attempt to retain the method while dispensing with the points of doctrine proved part of the undoing of Marxism in the Eastern bloc: method alone was not sufficient to sustain the political 'grand narrative' that propped up the various regimes there.

In fact, in his insistence on the primacy of method, Lukács comes tantalisingly close to postmodernising Marxism. Method is not narrative as such, and its tradition-challenging nature encourages a postmodern kind of scepticism towards what we might call the 'theology' of grand narrative: the tendency for doctrine to become an enclosed world with its own internal debates removed from all contact with everyday reality. Lukács is just as much an enemy of entrenched interests as the postmodernist movement, just as critical of allowing past doctrinal disputes to set the agenda for present-day practice. This side of Lukács is still well worth defending regardless of what has happened to Marxism in the interim.

Lenin: A study on the unity of his thought

The 1967 preface also makes reference to Lukács' Lenin study as part of the process whereby he overcame the contradictions and negative tendencies of *HCC*. Lukács notes that his major concern in *Lenin: A study on the unity of his thought*, published the year after *HCC*, was to portray his subject as 'a profound philosopher of praxis, a man who passionately transforms theory into practice, a man whose sharp attention is always focused on the nodal points where theory becomes practice, practice becomes theory' (p. xxxii). Lenin becomes a model of Marxist philosophy, the antidote to the ultra-Hegelian abstraction of *HCC*. On the basis of its vision of what a philosophy of praxis should entail, *LSUT* can still lay some claim to our attention, although it would be pointless to deny the work's hagiographic tone – 'Lenin is the greatest thinker to have been produced by the revolutionary working-class movement since Marx . . . in a world-historical sense *the only theoretician equal to Marx* yet produced by the struggle for the liberation of the proletariat.'[13] Lenin is depicted in these pages as a realist and a flexible, yet always dialectically correct, tactician whose Marxism is orthodox in the sense that Lukács calls for it to be in *HCC* – method inspired and non-doctrinal. Thus Lenin is no political utopian and is under no illusions about the nature of the human material with which he will have to build the socialist future. He is against any mechanistic or fatalistic interpretation of the dialectic, and is also willing to compromise if that is necessary to reach his political objectives, as long as any such compromise involves no clear breach with the fundamental principles and methods of Marxism. Lenin's flexibility combined with orthodoxy is to be seen in the fact that his life's work comprises 'the consistent application of the Marxist dialectic to the ever-changing, perpetually new phenomena of an immense period of transition', and in his awareness that the dialectic '*only exists as theory in and through this application*' (p. 87). The philosophy of praxis constitutes precisely that flexibility and concrete application of the dialectic. Lenin's ability to extend theory into the realm of the concrete is what distinguishes him from other Marxist political theorists including, one assumes, the Lukács of *HCC*, although it should be said that, as presented here, the Leninist concept of party – a disciplined force '*always a step in front* of the struggling masses to show them the way' (p. 35) – sounds remarkably similar to the Lukácsian concept of party in *HCC*.

Despite the tendency towards canonisation of Lenin (and the 1967 postscript continues the process), *LSUT* is valuable for what it reveals about Lukács' understanding of the philosophy of praxis. Marxism is not to be construed as an abstract metaphysics but as a philosophy that can be translated into direct political action; Lenin is taken to be a model of how this should be done, the theorist who 'always related all phenomena to their ultimate basis – *to the concrete actions of concrete (in other words class-conditioned) men in accordance with their real class interests*' (p. 79). Leninism becomes for Lukács the way out of the impasse that he felt himself to be in after *HCC*, and he will try to attain some of that supposed tactical flexibility in both his political writings and political actions of the 1920s. Whether the shift to a Leninist perspective represents anything other than a slight change of emphasis on Lukács' part, rather than the rejection of a false theoretical position as he likes to describe it later, is more open to question. Seen from a late twentieth-century vantage-point, the views expressed in *HCC* and *LSUT* look broadly similar.

The Young Hegel

YH continues Lukács' preoccupation with Marxism's Hegelian heritage and comes from the period when he was busily engaged in building up a dossier of studies on literary realism. There are similarities in approach between the realist studies and *YH*. In both cases Lukács shows himself to be concerned above all with the factor of historical process, and *YH* is in fact a very 'realist' interpretation of Hegel's development, in which great stress is laid on the impact of socio-political crises such as the French Revolution and its aftermath on Hegel's thought. Far from becoming entangled in the abstract reaches of Hegelian idealism, Lukács is keen to present Hegel as proto-Marxist in the way that he establishes links between classical English economics and the concerns of dialectical philosophy. This is Hegel Marxised, as the subtitle, *Studies in the relations between dialectics and economics*, would suggest. He may be open to criticism on the philosophical conclusions he draws from classical English economics, but Hegel is the only German thinker before Marx to make the connection, and for that reason alone he must be credited with being ahead of his time and a logical source for Marx. If Lukács is going to be criticised for being Hegelian, then he will demonstrate that Hegel can be reclaimed for Marxism. Hence his concern to argue that Hegel never became quite as politically reactionary in later life as many commentators insist: Lukács' Hegel is no precursor of Bismarck and the Prussianised German Empire of the late nineteenth century, which prepared the ground for the eventual triumph of fascism.[14]

Opinions are certainly divided on *YH*, a work that Lukács' biographer, Árpád Kadarkay, describes as monumental, Lichtheim as virtually worthless. *YH* traces Hegel's career from the early days in Berne through his Frankfurt and Jena periods to the production of *The Phenomenology of Mind*. Of critical influence in Hegel's early development was the French Revolution, and Lukács maintains that despite never being seduced by the more extreme left-wing views of the revolutionary period, Hegel remained convinced to the end of his life of the event's historical necessity, regarding it as the foundation of modern civil society. The political philosophy of his Berne period shows the influence of French revolutionary thought in its critical attitude towards Christianity (a religion Hegel believed destroys the moral autonomy of the individual in the phenomenon he called 'positivity') and its enthusiasm for antiquity, which is considered to be a living model for present-day society. Lukács notes the beginnings of Hegel's acute historical consciousness in his contrast of antiquity and Christianity, arguing that

> for all the mystification and tortuousness of his subjective idealism, he nevertheless had a very clear insight into the connection between modern individualism as an ideology and a life-style, and the actual fragmentation and impoverishment of human personality in the course of the medieval and post-medieval periods.[15]

Lukács also notes, however, that the force of Hegel's anti-religious argument is curbed by the fact that he is in effect wanting to replace one faith, Christianity, with the supposedly non-positive religion of the Greeks. Nevertheless, the influence of the French Revolution shines through in his writings of the period.

Frankfurt witnesses a decisive change in Hegel's thought as English economics comes to form a basic component of his understanding of history and society. Hegel's primary concern from this point onwards is man in civil society, and it is in Frankfurt that the dialectic first appears in his thought in the context of an inquiry into what the transition from feudal to bourgeois society involved. Lukács is to emphasise this concern with economics in order to rescue Hegel from the fate of being dubbed an irrationalist or 'Romantic' philosopher. While admitting that his subject can fall into a mystified idealism, Lukács agrees with Marx that the dialectical method can be observed to develop even among 'the manure of contradictions' (quoted, p. 202), which Hegel's researches naturally seem to generate.

The Frankfurt period is certainly full of contradictions, particularly, Lukács contends, with regard to Hegel's views on Christianity. Many commentators see this as a Christian and even mystical phase in Hegel's career, but Lukács wants to play this down and to search instead for ambivalences in Hegel's treatment of the Christian religion. He finds such ambivalences in Hegel's new introduction to a manuscript from the Berne period, *The Positivity of the Christian Religion* as well as in *The Spirit of Christianity*, arguing that passages glorifying Christianity have to coexist with others showing Hegel's continuing dislike of positivity. Lukács concludes that 'Hegel never felt so close emotionally to Christianity as at this time. But it would be a great error to infer from this a feeling of closeness is the same thing as a total doctrinal agreement with the tenets of Christianity' (p. 179). It is worth citing this material if only to counter Lichtheim's dismissal of *YH* on the grounds that its central thesis is 'that the youthful Hegel never went through a religious phase'.[16] Lukács may wish to emphasise contradiction at the expense of Christian belief, and it could even be argued that he overestimates contradiction in pursuit of a specific, Marxising, interpretation of Hegel, but he clearly does not deny a religious phase in Hegel's development – indeed, he goes so far as to admit that there is a consistent tendency to idealise religion running right throughout Hegel's writings. Not for the first time we see Lichtheim's prejudices preventing any properly balanced assessment of the work of Lukács' Moscow phase.

One might say that Lukács chooses to minimise the Christian element in Hegel's thought, but that he feels no need to exclude it entirely from his interpretation. The Marxisation of Hegel does not require him to go that far. Lukács is quite capable of locating progressive tendencies (which in Hegel's case equals a sense of historical process coupled with at least some awareness of the importance of economics in societal development) within a reactionary world-view, and in the studies on realism will find this to be almost the norm, with such nineteenth-century novelists as Scott, Balzac and Tolstoy all being categorised in this way. Neither Christianity nor philosophical idealism proves any bar to Hegel's burgeoning sense of the critical role of contradiction in human development, and his researches often compel him beyond his ideology, much as will be the case with the great realists cited above. (Lukács notes correspondences between Hegel and Balzac in particular when it comes to progressive tendencies.) We then have the paradox of Hegel's development as a thinker, 'the more he is driven to abandon the revolutionary ideals of his youth, the more resolutely he "reconciles" himself to the rule of bourgeois society and the less his thought reaches out to new possibilities – then the more powerfully and consciously the dialectic in him awakens' (p. 234). Despite certain ideological and philosophical limitations in the work of the early Hegel, we can still see the emergence of that unity of philosophy and history which is so typical of his mature writings. Lichtheim's accusation that the central thesis of *YH* involves a denial of what to a Marxist would be regressive tendencies hardly stands up to close analysis, and further suggests a serious misreading of Lukács' analytical method. Lukács is never one to shy away from acknowledging 'the manure of contradictions' in any thinker, and what he finally decides is that Hegel's philosophy is 'an amalgam of atheistic and theological tendencies' (p. 524), which is to locate the historical dialectic of the period within Hegel's thought rather than to regard him as anti-religious as such.

If he is able to accommodate Hegel's religiosity and shift from revolutionary to bourgeois ideals, what Lukács will not accept is the interpretation of Hegel as an irrationalist. To all intents and purposes at this point in Lukács' career irrationalism equals fascism, and in his eyes there is no saving grace to either. All attempts to assimilate Hegel to the Romantic 'philosophy of life' are bitterly resisted by Lukács, for whom assessments like that of the neo-Hegelian Richard Kroner, that 'Hegel is undoubtedly the greatest irrationalist known to the history of philosophy' (quoted, p. 297), are to be regarded as blatant falsifications of Hegel's actual position. Lukács argues that Hegel utterly rejected Romantic individualism, and he is clearly concerned to combat irrationalist revisions of the German intellectual heritage, which he considers one of the creeping evils of fascism, noting that Goethe too has been a subject for such revisionary activity. To turn Hegel into an irrationalist is to strike at the roots of what makes his philosophy so important for Marxism: the sense of historical process and the dialectic working within that process to provide a means of overcoming ideological contradictions over time. The need to prevent German philosophy, and literature, from falling into 'enemy hands' is a pressing one for Lukács in the late 1930s, as fascist domination in Europe is reaching new heights. Hegel has to be Marxised not just to protect Lukács' position within the communist world (his Hegelian associations left him a suspect figure in Moscow), but also as a gesture against the spread of fascist hegemony. The nature and extent of Hegel's historical consciousness is an ideological issue of some importance under these circumstances.

Against the irrationalist reading of Hegel, Lukács offers us an economist one, where Hegel is to be regarded as an early German disciple of Adam Smith. Hegel is held to demonstrate considerable insight into both the progressive and the dehumanising aspects of capitalism in his Jena writings, an insight that is all the more remarkable given the generally economically backward state of German society at the time. Lukács identifies some references to the alienating quality of industrial labour which suggest to him that Hegel had a rudimentary understanding of the problem of fetishism, although he is careful to state that these are glimmerings only: Hegel may prefigure Marx in his economic enquiries, but he is still an idealist who fails to draw the correct – that is, materialist – conclusions from his economic insights. At a certain point Hegel lapses back into 'the miasmas of idealism' (p. 363), and he remains prone to seeing human development in overly teleological terms; his conception of the dialectic, for example, has theological overtones and does not leave enough room for human agency, for men to 'make their own history' as Marxists would have it. 'The social preconditions of Hegel's philosophy', Lukács points out, 'forced it into an idealistic mould from the outset, and at the same time they set definitive limits to his understanding of the laws governing society and history, limits which only intensified the tendency towards idealism' (p. 395). This is the background against which Hegel's progressivism has to be viewed, and it is in the disjunction between the progressive and negative tendencies where Hegel's fascination lies for Lukács. Out of this disjunction grows the desire to turn Hegel 'right way up', the Marxist enterprise, the desire to materialise him and to purge the dialectic of both teleology and theology. Despite being a member of a socially and economically backward country, Hegel provides the foundations for the Marxist science of society. This is Hegel Marxised all right, but with due attention being paid to his limitations.

What the *Phenomenology of Mind* proceeds to do, in leading us through the various stages of development of 'spirit', is to take us to the very boundary of materialism,

> showing how the subject gradually wrests its content from substance, an idealistic formulation which yet contains the extremely materialistic idea that the development and the vitality of consciousness depend on the extent to which it is able to reflect objective reality.   (p. 473)

Even though Hegel takes capitalism to be the most progressive form of human development, the one best adapted to the needs of spirit, he still establishes the basis for the theory of Marxism since it is clear, to Marxists anyway, that not all the contradictions spirit encounters in the course of its historical development actually have been resolved by the advent of the capitalist stage. To Lukács it is a case of the Hegelian dialectic being confronted by the need to go further than the recognition of the existence of capitalist society into the multitude of contradictions that society generates, and it will be Marxism that takes on board that responsibility.

The Hegel we are left with after *YH* is a logical source for Marxism as well as a respectable subject of study for a Marxist philosopher living under a Soviet regime. The concern is to show that Hegel need not lead to the abstractness of reasoning found in *HCC*. It is not so much Hegel that is to blame, although Lukács is exceedingly careful to spell out Hegel's limitations as a dialectician in *YH*, but Lukács' somewhat uncritical use of his method in the earlier work. Purged of his idealist heresy, Lukács can proceed to identify what is worth retaining for Marxism from Hegel's early work, and that proves to be the progressivism within a reactionary framework, 'the manure of contradictions', which Lukács will also find to be the characteristic of the novels of the great realists of the nineteenth century. Hegel need no more be politically correct than any of the latter; it is his method, and the contradictions it generates, that is of interest. To his own satisfaction, Lukács has rehabilitated Hegel, as well as placed *HCC* in a different theoretical perspective. What remains contentious is whether Lukács is underestimating the Christian, and overestimating the economic element in Hegel's thought in order to achieve these objectives.

The Ontology of Social Being

Lukács returns to the Hegelian 'manure of contradictions' and its importance for the development of Marxism in the late, and posthumously published, *The Ontology of Social Being*. *OSB* is an attempt to re-establish contact with the great traditions of Marxism, taking the ontology of social being, from Hegel through Marx, as its theme, 'for in the present chaos of ingeniously distorted, superficially reductionist and falsely "profound" theories,' Lukács complains in similar vein to the *HCC* preface of 1967, 'the renovation of Marxism that is needed requires a well-founded and founding ontology that finds a real basis for social being in the objective reality of nature, and that is equipped to depict social being in its simultaneous identity and difference with nature.'[17] Working out the contradictions in the Hegelian dialectic is the first step in the process by which ontology will be reconstituted as a philosophy based on history. For a Marxist the ontological question is not 'x exists . . . how is it possible?' but 'x exists . . . what historical necessities brought it into being?' (*RL*, p. 164).

Lukács points to distortions in Hegel's ontology, which are the product of the methodological predominance of logic in his system of thought. In fact, Hegel's logic is from its inception a blending of logic and ontology, which precipitates him into some unfortunate philosophical myths such as the theory of the identical subject and object, 'which has to violate the basic ontological facts to achieve its intended unification of subject and object' (p. 28). It is not just Hegel who is under attack here, but the Lukács of *HCC* with his postulation of the proletariat as the identical subject–object of history – and behind that the new admirers of *HCC* of the 1960s whom Lukács was admonishing in the 1967 preface.

What to Lukács is a clear case of confusion between logical and ontological categories can be observed in Hegel's derivation of becoming from the dialectic of being and nothing. In point of fact, nothing is not to be regarded in its literal sense, but as what Hegel refers to as the 'not being of being other'. This is to blunt the role of negation in Hegel's ontology, since he is expressing 'what are really ontological categories, otherness and being-for-other, in logical language, while claiming to define the latter as a negation of being-in-itself' (p. 41). A logical nothing is therefore being illicitly equated with an ontological *relation*, which, as Lukács points out, contains no ontological element of negation within itself. Since Hegelian logic is critically dependent on the concept of the negation of the negation, the lack of any precise ontological equivalent has to be considered worrying when the theory is exposed to the real world.

Engels' celebrated analysis of the negation of the negation in biological terms (the 'negation' of the grain of barley by the barley plant that grows from it) merely succeeds in revealing the scale of the problem that Hegelian logic bequeaths us. Lukács argues that the grain of barley is in fact *annihilated* in the real world, and that 'this is the proper ontological expression for the term "negation", which has a definite logical meaning, but does not mean much ontologically' (p. 42). Subsuming a process like the annihilation of a grain of barley under the heading of logical negation only confuses matters. Furthermore, when one considers inorganic nature one finds not negation, 'but merely a chain of transformations from one form of being into another, a mere chain of relations in which each element has simultaneously an otherness and a being-for-other' (p. 43). In such cases it hardly seems permissible to continue to operate with the logical category of negation. Hegelian logic, which generalises negation into a fundamental moment of every dialectical process, therefore effectively destroys the specificity of social being.

When we turn to Marx, on the other hand, we find no such confusion between the logical and the ontological. Instead, he provides the basis for an ontological theory of the development of social being. The abstract complexes of the Hegelian totality are replaced in Marx by real complexes (the economic, for instance), 'involved with other real complexes in complicated and often very indirect reciprocal relationships'.[18] Marx is concerned with social practices, such as capitalist industrial production, rather than with abstract theory, and economics moves to the centre of his ontology, although Lukács is quick to point out that there is no mechanistic connection being assumed between economics and social being. Social being features a dialectic of economic and extra-economic factors in Marx, although the ultimately decisive factor is always the former: 'even the directly extra-economic transformations are in the last instance economically determined' (p. 67) Lukács notes, straying into that grey area of determinism which he is usually at such pains to avoid (the 'last instance' thesis being one of the least defensible positions in Marxist theory who-ever happens to invoke it). The class struggle under such a reading turns into 'a synthesis of economic law and extra-economic com-ponents of the same social reality' (p. 97), and socialism 'the nor-mal and necessary product of the internal dialectic of social being, of the self-development of the economy with all its presupposi-tions and consequences' (p. 159). Ontology always has a social basis in Marx, therefore, rather than the confusingly logical char-acter that it has in Hegel. Social being is a process firmly located in history, neither abstractly logical as Lukács conceived of it in *HCC*, nor crudely mechanistic in relation to the economy as the vulgar materialists or Stalinists would have it. (Marx allows for unequal development in the various sectors of ideology, a factor Lukács never loses sight of in his own cultural enquiries.) If we want to explain the phenomenon of the isolated individual in bourgeois culture, as evidenced, for example, in its many literary formulations from Robinson Crusoe to Kafka's K and the assorted anti-heroes of the modernist movement, we need to do so in his-torical rather than ontological terms.

The disposition to regard individual isolation or alienation as an ontological rather than a socio-historical phenomenon is one of the many sins of bourgeois ideology as well as of the literature that it nurtures. For Lukács it is an ideologically significant belief, effec-tively a way of deflecting protest against the dehumanising tenden-cies of capitalism, and that is invariably how it is dealt with in his analyses of modernism in literature. Philosophically speaking, one of the most notorious manifestations of the belief in the modern world is existentialism. Elsewhere Lukács is intensely critical of what he considers to be the moral nihilism of Sartre and his followers, whose concept of nothingness is merely 'a myth of declining capitalism' (*MHL*, p. 254). The only ones to benefit from the denial by intellectuals of the possibility of socio-historical orientation are the ruling bourgeoisie, who will hardly be troubled by the isolated, alienated egotists of existentialist ontology. What Lukács fails to acknowledge in his post-war polemic against Sartre is that the latter is just as exercised by the phenomenon of personal alienation as he is, and that he does take some steps to provide for its counteraction at the individual level with the concept of commitment, where individuals freely commit themselves to the rest of humanity through their actions (such as joining some cause like the Resistance and making its concerns one's own). Lukács is not really willing to give any philosophy which starts out from the individual 'abandoned' into existence much benefit of the doubt, and existentialism is dismissed as yet another sorry chapter in the long history of irrationalism in Western thought.

In a sense *OSB* is yet one more rejoinder to *HCC*, a book which casts a very long shadow in Lukács' career, and it can be regarded as part of the author's long drawn-out campaign to distance himself from the earlier work. In the 1967 preface Lukács remarks that his self-criticism of *HCC* caused him little pain because 'having once discarded any of my works I remain indifferent to them for the whole of my life' (*HCC*, p. xxxviii); but circumstances conspired to confront him again and again with the fact of *HCC*, and indeed we even find a group of his own students making an unfavourable comparison between *HCC* and *OSB* shortly after his death on the basis of disputes with him in his last years ('the author of *History and Class Consciousness*, whose radical rejection of his masterpiece we never shared').[19] While we might admire the almost postmodern refusal to be held back by his own 'grand narratives', as well as the endorsement of the 'death of the author' notion from an unexpected quarter, we might also wonder whether this is not an undialectical attitude to adopt towards Marxist cultural history. The history of *HCC*, a text with a proven ability to reveal deep fractures within both Marxist theory and the Marxist establishment, would suggest that an air of indifference is the one thing that cannot be maintained in the face of the notorious complexities of 'the Hegel problem' within Marxism.

The Destruction of Reason

DR generates little enthusiasm among Lukács' commentators, several referring to it as the author's worst book, for all that Lukács himself regarded it as one of his very best efforts.[20] Lichtheim, ever ready to condemn the later Lukács, goes so far as to claim that *DR*'s line of argument 'represents an intellectual crime'; by contrast H. A. Hodges considers that Lukács' presentation of the history of irrationalism is 'detailed and in many ways convincing' and Mészaros that there are are some 'really fine and gripping chapters' to note, despite the study's overall unevenness.[21]

The book is a lengthy critique of irrationalist tendencies in German thought from the age of Hegel to the age of Hitler, which holds thinkers like Schopenhauer, Nietzsche, Dilthey and Weber collectively responsible, even if only indirectly, for the development of Nazism and most of the ills of the modern world order. An epilogue carries the battle against unreason into post-war Western Europe and America as well. Germany's path to Hitler is traced through the history of post-Enlightenment German philosophy, which in Lukács' polemical account proves to be a series of reactionary responses to problems arising out of the depths of the class struggle, in which a host of figures is culpable of providing the cultural basis for the Hitler phenomenon: 'Everything that had been said on irrationalist pessimism from Nietzsche and Dilthey to Heidegger and Jaspers on lecture platforms and in intellectuals' salons and cafés, Hitler and Rosenberg transferred to the streets.'[22] Siding for or against reason in one's philosophy is a political act in Lukács' opinion, and to align oneself with irrationalism, to collude in the destruction of reason in human affairs, is effectively to take up arms against socialism in this highly biased survey of the German philosophical tradition, which is in no mood for compromise.

Irrationalism is condemned as 'the disparagement of understanding and reason, an uncritical glorification of intuition, the rejection of socio-historical progress, the creating of myths' (p. 10), all of which traits go to provide the bourgeoisie with philosophical 'comfort', and are to be found in particularly potent form in Nietzsche, a one-time significant influence on Lukács' thought but here reduced to the status of whipping-boy for anti-fascist polemic. Nietzsche is seen as the founder of irrationalism in the imperialist era and thus a precursor of Nazism and class enemy of Marxism and socialism. It matters little that Nietzsche did not read Marx or Engels; his philosophy is formed by the class struggle of his age and it reveals him to have 'a special sixth sense, an anticipatory sensitivity to what the parasitical intelligentsia would need in the imperialist age, what would inwardly move and disturb it, and what kind of answer would most appease it' (p. 315). The phenomenon that is involved here, as it is in thinkers like Schopenhauer, Dilthey and Weber too, is what Lukács calls 'indirect apologetics'. The destruction of reason these thinkers are engaged in serves the interests of capitalism by isolating and alienating the individual, thereby discouraging any collective action against capitalism and its excesses. Their philosophy therefore provides indirect succour for the capitalist cause, which benefits from an intellectual climate promoting passivity and acceptance of the intractable problems of an unchangeable 'human condition'. That is why Lukács proceeds to hymn the praises of the post-war peace movement, since it amounts to a mass uprising in the service of reason and as such is a counter to the institutionalised irrationalism of Western capitalism.

Lukács' account of irrationalist thought takes in pessimism, vitalism, social Darwinism, neo-Hegelianism, phenomenology and sociology along the way, all of which are seen to contribute in their own special manner to the softening up of the German character, which led to the triumph of Hitler and fascism. His fear in the 1950s is that irrationalism has simply transplanted itself in America and its allies, such that the Cold War has become yet another chapter in the modern world's titanic struggle between reason and unreason. Irrationalism runs deep in Western culture, and philosophy must take its share of the blame: 'Every thinker', Lukács warns, 'is responsible to history for the objective substance of his philosophizing' (p. 4), a verdict which allows no room for appeal in the case of someone like Nietzsche. One might wonder in passing whether the same 'responsibility to history' should also condemn Marx for the rise of Stalinism.[23]

While the sweep of *DR* is impressive, and while it also makes some perceptive points about the relationship between social being and consciousness, it declines into a diatribe against non-materialist philosophy, which is fairly crude by Lukács' normal standards of argument. We are asked to accept that all but a select band of approved materialists were suffering from false consciousness, and that the true, dialectical nature of reality discloses itself to few. The sheer complexity of historical process, which Lukács is usually so adept at conveying, is glossed over in favour of a very reductive interpretation of the development of German culture in which there seems to be a remorseless internal drive towards Hitlerism. Nazism is read back into Nietzsche's work in a very unhistorical way. Nietzsche has of late become something of a cult figure on the left, and although this phenomenon would probably only have confirmed Lukács in his distrust of Western intellectuals had he witnessed it in full flower, it also suggests that there need not be a one-to-one correspondence between Nietzschean philosophy and fascism. While one can understand, and also sympathise with, Lukács' desire for a settling of accounts with the legacy of German irrationalism, one would have to put a very large question-mark over *DR*'s way of prosecuting it. In the main, Lukács' dialectical subtlety deserts him here and the book has the air of a witch-hunt.

The Specificity of the Aesthetic

For Lukács there is an objective reality which exists independently of our consciousness (we do not, as such, *construct* the world) and irrationalism fails to portray that world correctly; that is, it fails to acknowledge that it is graspable by reason. Lukács takes it to be the task of art to reflect that reality existing independently of us in all its changing and developing nature, and his aesthetic theory, is firmly anchored in 'realism'. *The Specificity of the Aesthetic* (1963), one of Lukács' last complete works, codifies the theory underpinning the earlier realist studies, and we shall consider it briefly here as a prelude to our exploration of those same studies in chapters 3–6. It should be noted that reflection does not mean anything passive or mechanical in Lukács; aesthetic reflection is no mere copying of reality, more a case of laying bare the socio-historical processes that go to make reality what it is. Realistic reflection is one of the fundamental principles of Lukács' aesthetic theory, others being art as a special category, and the concepts of type and totality. For Lukács art is a special category located between the categories of the individual (the here-and-now) and the universal (the essential). In this in-between category of specialty, art can create a world that is both typical and total. Typicality involves mediating between the individual and the universal, so that a typical character in a realist novel will be seen as having to respond in her own personal way to the large-scale socio-historical forces unfolding around her;

to be a typical individual is to synthesise the individual and the universal in one's person, as is the case with Edward Waverley in Scott's novel *Waverley*, for example. The work of art constitutes a self-enclosed totality different from, though in relation to, reality, which enables us to see more deeply *into* reality.

Lukács identifies three basic signalising systems in human communication: primary, secondary and primary-plus. The first involves something like Pavlovian conditioned reflex; the second is our ordinary language system; and the last is between the other two, effectively the language of art in its category of specialty. The primary-plus system also includes intuition and the unconscious, since these are both part of Lukács' extended concept of rationality. Thus authors can be praised for reflecting things that are not present in their conscious intention, for unwittingly revealing what their socio-political prejudices would rather keep hidden (Scott, Balzac and Tolstoy will be particularly singled out for such treatment). Subtexts are an integral part of the primary-plus system and one of the major reasons why art is such a valuable area of human activity: in art-works we can read what reality actually is and not what our political masters (be they bourgeois or Stalinist) say it should be. Art-works which fail to synthesise the individual and the universal hide reality from us, allegory being a prime example of such failure, in that it involves the author seeking to make the universal contain the special rather than the other way round: this is the objection Lukács makes to Kafka's works *The Trial* and *The Castle*, when he analyses their narrative world in *MCR*. When the universal is contained in the special we have symbolism, which promotes a greater understanding of reality. The whole purpose of the aesthetic effect, which Lukács conceives of in a more or less cathartic way, is to reach this level of greater understanding. If we do not have precisely this aesthetic effect, then we do not have art. Aesthetic value is the ability of an art-work to recreate the aesthetic effect over time – Scott, Balzac and Tolstoy all show how this can be done.

As mentioned before, these aesthetic principles constitute a further level of conceptualisation of the ideas informing Lukács' middle-period criticism, and we shall return to them when we come to consider in more detail Lukács' work on literary realism. What we can note about the late aesthetics, in common with all Lukács' writings on Marxist philosophy, is an overriding concern

with totality and historical process. Regardless of the various re-
tractions of his early efforts as a Marxist philosopher which
Lukács was to be engaged in, there is that thread of continuity
running from *HCC* through to the late writings on aesthetics and
ontology.

Theory and criticism:
early works

We turn now to the most significant works of Lukács' pre-Marxist phase, *Soul and Form* and *The Theory of the Novel*, works of critical and aesthetic theory, which are strongly idealist in character and marked by a sense of extreme pessimism, in sharp contrast to the tone of the later Marxist critical studies.[1] As Lukács himself notes in his 1962 preface to *TN*, 'it was written in a mood of permanent despair over the state of the world. It was not until 1917 that I found an answer to the problems which, until then, had seemed to me insoluble' (p. 2). It was in 1917, of course, that Lukács began to fall under the spell of Marxism.

Soul and Form

To come to a work like *SF* through Lukács' Marxist reputation – Lukács the staunch defender of realism, the insistent advocate of literature's sociological and ideological significance – can be something of a shock. Here in this collection of essays is a world-view that seems to owe more to the modernism that Lukács was later to criticise so vehemently than one would have thought possible, a world-view permeated by the pessimism so fashionable in Central European intellectual and artistic circles before the First World

War: 'Life is an anarchy of light and dark: nothing is ever completely fulfilled in life, nothing ever quite ends; new, confusing voices always mingle with the chorus of those that have been heard before.'[2] This is historical process without any particular direction or ultimate point (René Wellek notes an existentialist character to the work's outlook),[3] and it is a world away from the author's later, optimistic (in the Marxist sense), conception of historical process as an arena in which people can come to understand, and also come to shape, their own destiny. Counterposed to the anarchy of life is the form-giving world of art. Artistic form is seen to have a spiritual quality in *SF*; it is a way of bringing order to chaos: 'Form is the highest judge of life. Form-giving is a judging force, an ethic; there is a value-judgement in everything that has been given form' (p. 173). Form almost becomes the point of life under such a reading and form-giving the highest state of consciousness, but form is also held to be the most transitory of phenomena. In a passage almost worthy of Derrida, Lukács argues: 'Every written work leads toward great moments in which we can suddenly glimpse the dark abysses into whose depths we must fall one day; and the desire to fall them is the hidden content of our lives' (p. 113). Deconstruction is quite at home with abysses and writing as a disruptive force (viz. Derrida, 'Writing is the moment of this original Valley of the other within Being. The moment of depth as decay'),[4] although it does not have the same faith in form as a way of arresting the drive towards instability. It is odd to be able to place Lukács in such company, however briefly, and one can only speculate on how he might have developed had not Marxism intervened.

Those isolated moments of understanding that form gives us constitute the focus of the critic's attention, and great claims are made for the critical role: 'The critic is one who glimpses destiny in forms: whose most profound experience is the soul-content which forms indirectly and unconsciously conceal within themselves' (p. 8). Although the terminology is rather high-flown, intimations of the later Lukács' critical practice can be noted here. As a Marxist critic he is invariably concerned with what literary forms can reveal about *ideological* destiny; thus realism is to be prized for the glimpses it offers of the soul-content, that is, the essence, of its informing ideology. Criticism is conceived of as a creative activity in *SF*, and the critical essay just as much an act of form-giving as novel writing or poetry writing is. The critic, no less than the novelist or poet, orders the confusing voices that surround us and gives glimpses of the abysses that await us. To put this in modern terms of reference, the critical narrative can be as valuable as the fictional one: both are to be regarded as ways of organising experience, of giving form to disparate and chaotic material. Lukács might overstate the case – the critic is even described as being like 'a Homeric hero' (p. 24) – but his conception of the critical function is not as far-fetched as it might at first appear to be. Certainly the Lukácsian critical narrative as a whole can be defined as 'form-giving'.

If there are intimations of the later Lukács in the earlier on the subject of the critical function, the matter is very different when it comes to world-views. The Lukács of *SF* is essentially a pessimist who can speak of 'the unbridgeable void between one human being and another' (p. 107), and is irresistibly drawn to the work of Kierkegaard. The inescapable conclusion is that ordinary life lacks form ('we experience ourselves only peripherally' there, Lukács complains (p. 157)), and we therefore look to art and criticism, the world of forms, to supply the lack and give some sense of meaning to existence: 'This is the most profound meaning of form: to lead to a great moment of silence, to mould the directionless, precipitous, many-coloured stream of life as though all its haste were only for the sake of such moments' (p. 114). The idea of literature as a source of refuge from reality is one that Lukács is shortly to repudiate altogether in favour of a sociological approach to the subject, where it is the relationship between literary activity and historical process that is significant. A considerable gulf separates *SF* from post-1917 Lukács, therefore, although it is worth noting that 'realism' will take on many of the talismanic qualities earlier associated with form.

The Theory of the Novel

TN is even more pessimistic in tone as befits a work written in a mood of deep personal despair at the outbreak of the First World War (the book was completed in the winter of 1914–15). Lukács describes his attitude at the time as 'one of vehement, global and, especially at the beginning, scarcely articulate rejection of the war and especially of enthusiasm for the war' (Preface, 1962, p. 11).

This surfaces in the book's anti-bourgeois stance of extreme pessimism towards the present age, an age in which the novel, that 'epic of a world that has been abandoned by God' (p. 88), as Lukács gloomily terms it, becomes the representative art-form and irony its appropriate tone. What the novel comes to delineate, Lukács remarks in his most despairing vein, is a world where 'man became lonely and could find meaning and substance only in his own soul, whose home was nowhere' (p. 103).

TN establishes Lukács' lifelong obsession with the novel, and particularly with the subject of the novel's historicity. Although it contains traces of several intellectual influences – Lukács cites Dilthey, Simmel, Weber, Sorel, Schlegel, Solger and Kierkegaard as part of his intellectual baggage at the time – Hegel is clearly the dominant methodological guide for *TN*'s historicisation of literary forms. The book's concern is to map out literature's journey from the epic to the novel in a more or less Hegelian manner, with the author seeking to work out a dialectic of literary genres which can account for the novel's current dominance. The terms of reference are somewhat abstract, and, as Jameson points out, over-dependent on 'a kind of literary nostalgia' for a supposed golden age of Greek epic narrative,[5] but there is a sense of historical process throughout *TN* that is largely missing from *SF*'s more rarefied argument. Certainly, the issue of form is approached in a noticeably more dialectical way:

> The epic and the novel, these two major forms of great epic literature, differ from one another not by their authors' fundamental intentions, but by the given historico-philosophical realities with which the authors were confronted. The novel is the epic of an age in which the extensive totality of life is no longer directly given, in which the immanence of meaning in life has become a problem, yet which still thinks in terms of totality. (p. 56)

The ahistorical conception of form in *SF* is replaced by a Hegelian recognition that 'Every form is the resolution of a fundamental dissonance of existence' (p. 62). *TN*'s brief is to trace the history of that existential dissonance to which the novel is a response; and for all its Hegelianised abstraction, there is a real feeling of historical consciousness at work here, which signals the direction in which Lukács ultimately was to head.

The epic and the novel are presented as the forms of childhood and virile maturity respectively, which dictates that the former historically must yield to the latter as our concept of life and the nature of being changes. Greek epic is the product of a closed, and simpler, world and gives form to that world's totality of life. It is a world with a stable system of values, which everyone understands, even if some individuals may transgress against them. Epic mimics its moral straightforwardness and lack of ontological or ideological complexity:

> The epic world is either a purely childlike one in which the transgression of stable, traditional norms has to entail vengeance which again must be avenged *ad infinitum*, or else it is the perfect theodicy in which crime and punishment lie in the scales of world justice as equal, mutually homogeneous weights. (p. 61)

The rift between inside and outside, self and world, which marks out the individual's experience in modern times, is missing in the epic context, whose hero is never really an individual but rather a community. In such a stable value-system, where the nature of being hardly comes under scrutiny, there is to be no 'polemical self-contemplation by the lost and lonely personality' but simply a series of adventures whose significance relates 'to a great organic life complex – a nation or a family' (p. 67). In the novel, on the other hand, it is precisely the experience of that 'lost and lonely personality' in problematical relationship to her world with which we have to deal. The forms mark the difference between a world that is organic and stable and one that is contingent and discrete, between a world in which everyone shares a sense of social destiny and one in which they no longer do.

Dante represents a transitional phase between the epic and the novel, his being the landscape of epic in terms of its totality of conception, but a landscape peopled by figures standing in a problematic relationship to that totality. His characters begin to register as individuals working out their own rather than any social destiny, and we are gradually drawn into their psychology in a way that we never are with the heroes of the classical epic. If not quite lost and lonely personalities on the modern model, Dante's characters, or at least some of them, have lost that unselfconscious relationship to reality that was the hallmark of the true epic hero. We have structural principles tending towards the novel in Dante, even if these are ultimately kept within the bounds of the epic form. The totality of Christian doctrine underpins the Dantean narrative for all the individuality of his characters. It is when this particular totality begins to decline that the novel is born; with *Don Quixote* we have crossed the line that divides epic from novel:

> Thus the first great novel of world literature stands at the beginning of the time when the Christian God began to forsake the world; when man became lonely and could find meaning and substance only in his own soul, whose home was nowhere; when the world, released from its paradoxical anchorage in a beyond that is truly present, was abandoned to its immanent meaninglessness.   (p. 103)

This is a rather complicated way of saying that the novel marks the shift from feudal to bourgeois culture and that it is to be considered as a response to the break-up of the Catholic totality of doctrine (the Protestant Reformation) in the first instance, and then the progressive decline of Christian belief over the following centuries. However abstractly stated, we can observe connections being forged between literary form and historical process in a recognisably dialectical way.

The novel is, therefore, the product of a new cultural sensibility, the art-form of virile maturity. To be such an art-form is to present a world whose apparent completeness is an illusion; thus the novel appears as a form always in the process of becoming ('a hybrid form which must be reinvented at every moment of its development,' as Jameson puts it),[6] and as 'the epic of an age in which the extensive totality is no longer given . . . yet which still thinks in terms of that totality' (p. 56). The novel deals with the progress of that lost and lonely individual in a contingent world where cultural certainties either have collapsed or are in the act of collapsing, and it is an outwardly biographical form whose inner form is the process of the individual's journey towards self-recognition. In the journey through this contingent world the most the individual can hope for is occasional glimpses of meaning. While she may come to realise this will have to suffice to justify the commitment of her entire life, a sense of melancholy often attaches itself to this realisation:

> The melancholy of the adult state arises from our dual, conflicting experience that, on the one hand, our absolute, youthful confidence in

an inner voice has diminished or died, and, on the other hand, that the outside world to which we now devote ourselves in our desire to learn its ways and dominate it will never speak to us in a voice that will clearly tell us our way and determine our goal.   (p. 86)

There is a clear loss of the sense of social destiny that characterised the world of the epic, and of the security that went along with it; faced with contingency and with a nostalgia for a totality which can never be recovered, the condition of the novel hero is more likely to be one of insecurity. The discrepancy between the world as it is and the world as it should be is the source of the irony that makes the novel the most representative art-form of its age:

the antagonistic nature of the inner and outer worlds is not abolished but only recognised as necessary; the subject which recognises it as such is just as empirical – just as much part of the outside world, confined in its own interiority – as the characters which have become its objects. . . . In the novel the subject, as observer and creator, is compelled by irony to apply its recognition of the world to itself and to treat itself, like its own creatures, as a free object of free irony.   (p. 75)

The tragedy of the modern world which the novel so clearly delineates is the simultaneous presence in the individual of a desire to unify the inner and outer worlds in the manner of the classical epic, and the recognition that this is no longer possible, that the cultural conditions which sustained such a unity are gone beyond recall.

After the highly abstract arguments of part I of *TN* Lukács moves, by way of a projected typology of the novel form, into criticism of actual texts in part II. The basis of the typology is the incommensurability of inner and outer reality in the aftermath of God's abandonment of the world, and it divides into two main forms: either the leading character's soul is 'too narrow' or it is 'too broad' in relation to the outside world. Corresponding to the division are novels of abstract idealism or romantic disillusionment. In abstract idealism we note a narrowing of the soul of the hero, who, consumed by the desire to realise some ideal, blames reality when it cannot be achieved. This is the case of Don Quixote. The inadequacy of the relation between hero and outside world is a source of great comedy in Cervantes, who skilfully blends the sublime and the ridiculous to prevent his character from becoming a mere grotesque. Dickens provides no such counterweight of the sublime, substituting instead the bourgeois concept of decent behaviour; thus his novels, rich though they are in comic characters and humorous examples of narrowing of the soul, are, in the final analysis, it is felt, flat and moralistic. Balzac, however, escapes such a charge, giving us a narrative world peopled exclusively by narrow souls perpetually at cross-purposes with each other; as a result, 'we obtain that strange, boundless, immeasurable mass of interweaving destinies and lonely souls which is the unique feature of Balzac's novels' (p. 108).

The novel of disillusionment deals with the other type of incommensurability: when the soul proves to be wider than any of the destinies that life has to offer it. The tendency in such novels is for the protagonist to retreat into an inner world whose psychological depth and richness are preferred to the stifling conventionalism of the outer world of society. Lukács is critical of such intense interiorisation of experience, with its mood of disillusioned romanticism and effective abandonment of any claim to engage in the shaping of the social world, and finds an inner emptiness in this kind of narrative. Flaubert and C. F. Meyer (both of whom are to be subjected to even more severe critique in Lukács' later Marxist studies) are identified as prime exponents of the disillusionment style, although the former's *L'Education sentimentale* is considered, against the odds, to attain a sense of epic objectivity. (Similar noises are made about Tolstoy too.) The novel of disillusionment continually flirts with formlessness, although it can overcome this danger to a certain extent by the use of time as a structuring device. Lukács anticipates the narrative practice of writers such as Proust and Joyce in his remarks on time and the novel, particularly in the references to the structural opportunities afforded by the Bergsonian concept of *durée* (the duration experienced time of consciousness as opposed to the mathematically conceived time of physics).

The novel of disillusionment is taken to be the current limit of literary development, and Lukács' gloomy prognosis that no new type is on the horizon is of a piece with his intensely pessimistic reading of the European socio-political situation at the time. Drawing on Fichte, he observes despondently that the 'novel is the form of the epoch of absolute sinfulness . . . and it must remain the dominant form so long as the world is ruled by the same stars'

(p. 152). In 1914–15 Lukács can see very little prospect of that state of affairs coming to an end. A fairly straightforward correlation between literature and historical process is assumed, in which literary forms are held to be bound to their historical moment, and given an ideology of disillusionment a novel of disillusionment almost naturally follows. Lukács has reached a dead end with his Hegelianised conception of historical process, which allows him to see no particular hope for the future. He stands on the verge of the modernist problematic, with its essentially pessimistic view of the human condition at the close of *TN*, but that will be as far as he goes. Marxism will enable him to overcome disillusionment and to adopt a different perspective entirely on literary history and historical process, a perspective which will insist that 'man makes his own history' and is no mere victim of brute historical forces outside all possible human control. This is not to minimise the importance of *TN*, which remains a very powerful document of the pessimistic strain in modern European culture, but rather to suggest that it exhausts one particular line of development in Lukács' thought. Henceforth in Lukács' writings on literature world-weariness and cloudy metaphysics are out, political commitment and concrete social analyses are in, and we are to find some strikingly different readings of the authors treated in part II of *TN* in his subsequent Marxist phase.

| CHAPTER THREE | *The theory of realism* |

Before going on to work our way through the major studies on realism of Lukács' Marxist phase it is worth our while to consider briefly the principles underpinning his theory of literary realism. A useful means of doing so is provided by two essays from the 1930s in the collection *Writer and Critic*: 'Narrate or Describe?' and 'The Intellectual Physiognomy in Characterisation'. These both appeared in 1936 and give us the main lines of the theory to be elaborated in more detail in the various textual studies of Lukács' maturity (and later codified in *SA*). The essays tell us what realism should involve in terms of characterisation and narrative form, point to examples of good and bad practice from a realist perspective, and suggest some nineteenth-century models for the contemporary novel to follow.

'Narrate or Describe?'

'Narrate or Describe?' postulates two main ways of organising narrative material: active narration or passive description. In the former there is careful selection of detail such that the significance of each scene in terms of the overall narrative structure is clear, in the latter a mass of descriptive detail only very loosely, if at all, connected to the plot and the narrative drive. Only when we are in the presence of narration, Lukács contends, do we become properly involved as readers in the action taking place. Lukács cites similar scenes in Zola's *Nana* and Tolstoy's *Anna Karenina* as representative instances of the two contrasting approaches to narrative form. In each case a horse race is being depicted, but it is only in *Anna Karenina* that the scene can be said to further the narrative or deepen our understanding of the significance of the characters' lives. The crucial difference in Lukács' view is that whereas Zola merely describes the scene, Tolstoy narrates it. Zola deluges us with a profusion of descriptive detail concerning the race in what is conceded to be a virtuoso display of writing technique. Every aspect of the race, from the saddling of the horses through to its finish, is meticulously recorded, yet the overall scene is largely irrelevant to the progress of the plot; all it establishes is that one of Nana's numerous casual lovers is ruined in a betting fraud connected with the race and it could easily be eliminated, being little better than a narrative filler, in Lukács' opinion. In *Anna Karenina*, on the other hand, the race represents a crisis point in the lives of the novel's main characters and is an integral part of the action. Vronsky needs to win the race to revive his failing military career, which has been held back in part by his liaison with Anna, and his subsequent fall in the race is a catastrophic event not just for him but for Anna also, whose shock at Vronsky's misfortune causes her to reveal their hitherto clandestine relationship to her husband. All the details Tolstoy gives us of the preparations for the race and the events of the race itself are therefore necessary to communicate the importance of what is occurring for the characters' lives; the details are carefully selected by the author to make the audience realise that we are at a turning-point in the plot. The horse race is used, therefore, to bring a particular narrative structure to a head and not just as a means to display literary virtuosity for its own sake: 'In Zola the race is *described* from the standpoint of an observer; in Tolstoy it is *narrated* from the standpoint of the participant.'[1] Which is to say that Zola is a naturalist and Tolstoy a realist, Zola a warning to the modern novelist of where he or she can go wrong in the organisation of fictional material, Tolstoy a model for narrative practice.

Description for Lukács is a retrograde development in the history of the novel, a symptom of social and ideological decline:

'Description . . . becomes the dominant mode in composition in a period in which, for social reasons, the sense of what is primary in epic construction has been lost. Description is the writer's substitute for the epic significance that has been lost' (p. 127). The villain of the piece is capitalism with its dehumanising tendencies; description is a product of this development, a literary analogue to capitalism's levelling of human experience and crushing of the individual spirit. Narration, however, helps to keep us aware of the socio-political processes that shape us as individuals: 'Narration establishes proportions, description merely levels' (p. 127). Once these proportions are established, the author can set about the real task of all great epic art, the novel included, which is to discover the significant and vital elements of social practice. Realist narration is considered to be a way of keeping human values alive within the hostile environment that is modern capitalism. Choosing to remain at the level of description constitutes almost a moral failing on the author's part, a refusal to think through the dynamics of one's world-view. There is in effect a passive capitulation to capitalism in the descriptive method, which gives little sense of the complex and contradictory quality of the individual's relationship to the capitalist system. Naturalism is a precursor of modernism in terms of moral failure, and both will invariably come under attack from Lukács in the various studies on realism to follow.

'The Intellectual Physiognomy in Characterisation'

'The Intellectual Physiognomy in Characterisation' spells out what is required to achieve realist characterisation, and what is missing in this respect in naturalism and all other forms of literary 'decadence'. The emphasis is on the need for characters to be a conjunction of social and individual traits: 'Universal typical phenomena', Lukács urges, 'should emerge out of the particular actions and passions of specific individuals' (p. 154). 'Typicality' holds the key to successful characterisation and it demands that all characters must be granted a fully developed 'intellectual physiognomy' of their own, which distinguishes them from their fellows without damaging their status as representative products of their culture and its ideology. Their actions, narrated rather than described, should further our understanding of that culture and its ideology, and the greater the density of the interactions and interconnections between such 'typical' individuals over the course of the narrative, the greater the significance the novel will have as a picture of its time. The novel will become a self-enclosed totality operating in the category of specialty. Balzac and Tolstoy provide us with such density; Zola and Flaubert do not. In the case of the latter two their descriptive method, with its concentration on the details of day-to-day existence, hides the workings of ideology from us, thus reducing the significance of their narratives. 'Profound understanding of life', Lukács assures us, 'is never restricted to the observation of everyday existence' (p. 158). Without typicality there is no hope of the novel discharging its obligation to discover the significant and vital elements of social practice, and typicality depends on *selection* of observed detail:

> Of course, the old writers began with fragments of life they had experienced or observed. But by extracting these events out of the immediate context and re-ordering and modifying them according to their needs, they were able so to represent that subtle dependence of their characters on each other and their interaction with each other as to permit their characters to live out their lives in full creative richness. (p. 171)

A classic example of this art of extracting out of context can be found in *Don Quixote*, where Cervantes can transform a bizarre act like tilting at windmills (hardly an everyday occurrence) into one of the most typical scenes in world literature, one that tells us something valuable about an entire culture and not just the individual performing the action. Gorki displays a similar ability to discover the typical in the bizarre and exceptional. All writers face a mass of detail when they set about organising a narrative, realists are those with the talent to select with an eye to typicality.

The idea is building up that realism has to capture a sense of social process and that this can only be done by painstaking selection of detail, construction of characters who unite social and individual traits in their personality, and narration undertaken from the protagonists' perspective. If these procedures are adhered to, then we have typicality and the landscape of realism; if not, one or other form of literary decadence. Balzac and Tolstoy emerge from these pages as models for novel-writing; Flaubert and Zola as warnings of what can happen when the correct balance of social and individual is not maintained. The psychologism of a Flaubert and the naturalism of a Zola are traps for the writer to avoid: in the former case there is too little reflection of reality; in the latter, too much, although that does leave us, as Peter Demetz has pointed out, with the difficulty that 'the decision between what is too little and what is too much is unfortunately made not by the artist himself but by the socially committed philosopher'.[2] With form-giving, the theory-wielding critic has edged ahead of the author.

The principles of a theory of literary realism are now in place (to provide the basis for *SA* at a later date) and we have an agenda for the novel to address. We can now go on to consider the elaboration of this theory in Lukács' major studies on realism from the 1930s through to the 1960s.

Defending realism: (1) middle period works

The middle period of Lukács' career saw him producing a large volume of essays on literary realism, which would later appear in various post-war collections, and *The Historical Novel*, a pioneering work in Marxist aesthetics in terms of tracing the relationship between literary form and socio-economic development. Over the course of these writings Lukács mounts a spirited defence of the realist tradition in European literature, a tradition which he traces back to classical times, insisting firmly on Marxism's respect for the classical heritage of mankind. Defending realism, the paradigm of Marxist aesthetics in the period (although there was a strong modernist-minded counter-movement to it to which we shall be returning in chapter 7), becomes the overriding concern of Lukács' critical writings, right through to his late championship of Solzhenitsyn as the inheritor of all that is best in European realism and the standard-bearer for a projected new wave of realist literature. It is important to note that Lukács has a considerably more flexible concept of realism than most Marxist theorists of the time, although this very flexibility creates its own problems which need to be confronted. Over the next three chapters we shall be following the trajectory of this obsessive defence of realism and the problems that come in its wake.

In this chapter we shall be looking in detail at *Studies in European Realism* and *The Historical Novel*, with briefer excursions into

Essays on Realism and *Goethe and his Age* along the way. These are works written in a time of political turmoil in Europe with fascism in the ascendancy, and it is against this background, never far from the author's thoughts, that Lukács attempts to stake out a role for realism in socialism's crusade against its enemies. Literature is to be held ideologically accountable, an area into which the struggle against fascism legitimately can be extended.

Studies in European Realism

SER consists of a series of essays written in the 1930s when Lukács was resident in Moscow, and published as a representative compilation of his work on realism in the period in an English edition of 1950. The collection constitutes a sociological survey of the writings of major European authors such as Balzac, Stendhal, Zola, Tolstoy and Gorki, and it contains most of the dominant motifs that mark out Lukács' writings on realism. Thus we see the postulation of 1848, the year of European-wide social unrest and revolution which spawned *The Communist Manifesto*, as a crucial watershed in the development of European literary consciousness; the advocacy of certain key authors over others for aesthetic-ideological reasons (Balzac, Stendhal, Tolstoy and Gorki over Flaubert, Hugo and Zola, for example); the insistence, so radical from within the Marxist camp in the heyday of socialist realist aesthetics, that outward political affiliation does not necessarily determine aesthetic progressiveness ('reactionary traits in the world-view of great realist writers do not prevent them from depicting social reality in a comprehensive, correct and objective way,' in Lukács' emphatic words);[1] the concern to disclose the underlying sociological conditions for aesthetic productions, that is, the material roots of literature as a cultural phenomenon; the tendency to polarise aesthetic debate into sharply defined binary oppositions of the 'narrate or describe' kind (Balzac *or* Flaubert, as it will later be Kafka *or* Mann in *MCR*); and above all the unshakeable conviction in realism's social utility. 'Never in all history did mankind so urgently require a realist literature as it does today' (p. 18), Lukács asserts. That is to be a sentiment that echoes throughout his writings on realism.

Lukács' prefatory remarks from 1948 make clear the character of the critical consciousness informing his researches into realism: 'Marxism searches for the material roots of each pheno-menon, regards them in their historical connection and move-ment . . . and in so doing lifts every phenomenon out of a merely emotional, irrational, mystic fog and brings it to the light of understanding' (p. 1). The desire to discover how literature func-tions dynamically within a material context becomes the centre of Lukács' enquiry into the nature of literary realism, with the emphasis lying on showing how an earlier realist literature can continue to be a source of important knowledge to a modern audience. 'Marxism is not a Baedeker of history,' Lukács warns (p. 4), and *SER*'s essays are not designed for escapism-minded passive consumers of Europe's literary heritage: the older realism is presented as a cause well worth fighting for in terms of its continued usefulness in the class struggle. Lukács is at pains to dismiss the post-realist tradition, which he considers essentially decadent. The older realism is seen as an antidote to this de-cadence, whereas from 1848 onwards we can chart the steady decline of European literature, first into the 'novel of disillusion-ment' (which would seem to preach the hopelessness of the indi-vidual's plight), and then into what Lukács regards as the emptiness and ideologically suspect quality of modernism – a theme to be explored in more detail in *MCR*.

Lukács' treatment of Balzac, one of the heroes of his materialist revision of European literary history, is a model of his critical approach in this period. There is no attempt to play down Balzac's political conservatism, and his reactionary tendencies are freely admitted. Balzac's great virtue in Lukács' eyes is that despite his conservatism, and what is almost as bad a trait as far as a Marxist critic is concerned, his periodic utopianism, he contrives neverthe-less to reveal the true state of society at the time of writing. He is able 'to uncover the great social and economic forces which govern historical development' (p. 42). Even if Balzac never actually does this in a direct fashion, he is to be admired for the basic honesty of his outlook, whose clarity of vision invariably triumphs over his socio-political prejudices. Building on Marx's approving judge-ment of Balzac as a writer displaying a deep understanding of the real conditions of society, Lukács proceeds to turn the French novelist into a heroic figure in terms of France's social develop-ment, in spite of the 'discrepancy between intention and perfor-mance' (p. 21) plainly visible in Balzac's fiction.

Perhaps one should say *because* of that perceived discrepancy, since it is in precisely this gap that the materialist critic goes to work with a vengeance. In this respect Lukács can be regarded as an early exponent of 'reading against the grain', of the art of digging beneath the surface of a narrative to discover what it – unwittingly – discloses about the social relations of its time. When at a later point in Marxist literary-critical history Pierre Machérey recommends the materialist critic to search for 'the real debate' hidden behind authorial 'false resolutions' in a text, he is following in the footsteps of Lukács.[2] For all his reactionary beliefs Balzac is held to display a 'profound comprehension of the contradictorily progressive character of capitalist development' (p. 13) and its implications for human relations, which Lukács feels moved to applaud, arguing that the real subject of Balzac's novels is the triumph of capitalism. Balzac is taken, therefore, to present French society as it really is and not as his socio-political preju- dices would have it to be, the realist in him triumphing over the conservative. No higher compliment can be paid to a bourgeois author by a Marxist critic.

The subtlety of Lukács' handling of Balzac's *oeuvre* – and sub- tlety is surely the right word to use when we compare his critical method to that of socialist realism or the vulgar Marxism Lukács so often railed against – is revealed when we compare his reading of the politically reactionary Balzac to the politically radical Zola. On the face of it Zola, a progressive thinker who was never an apologist for the bourgeois social order as Lukács readily admits, ought to be the one to engage a Marxist's sympathies the more: this is, after all, the Zola who was a tireless campaigner in his novels against the evils of unchecked capitalist development in France and against corruption in French public life (consider his well-publicised role in the Dreyfus case). Yet while acknowledging his many virtues as a social observer, Lukács is ultimately highly critical of Zola's world-view, detecting an artistic falsity in his narrative method of naturalism which is regressive compared to Balzac's dispassionate view of capitalism and its many contradic- tions. Zola's critique may be sincere and acute, but it is also fatally 'locked into the magic circle of progressive *bourgeois* narrow- mindedness' (p. 87). Sincerity, it would seem, is not in itself enough to guarantee aesthetic success – a point perhaps lost on the more vociferous apologists for socialist realism at the time, who were not noted for their skill at digging beneath the surface of narratives in such thorough fashion. Just as reactionary traits in the world-view of a writer do not prevent her from depicting social reality in the required comprehensive, correct and objective way, so progressive traits, no matter how sincerely manifested, cannot be taken to guarantee a comprehensive, correct and objective picture of a writer's society either.

Even Stendhal, who impresses Lukács enough to pair him with Balzac as one of the two greatest realists of the nineteenth century, must rank behind the latter figure, possessor though he is of a confused and often downright reactionary world-view, when it comes to mirroring faithfully the social trends of the period 1789–1848. As with Zola, the republican-minded Stendhal seems the more likely recipient of Marxist approval, but for all his undoubted admiration of Stendhal's achievements, Lukács has no qualms at placing the monarchist Balzac higher in his list of literary heroes.

One of the areas where Lukács finds most discrepancy between Balzac and Zola is that of characterisation; indeed characterisation – the ability to create memorable types as Lukács conceives of it – is taken to constitute one of the distinguishing marks of great realist writing. Lukács goes so far as to say that 'the central aesthetic problem of realism is the adequate presentation of the complete human personality' (p. 7). (It is one of the many problems in defending Lukács on realism that he has a tendency to fall back on such loose criteria as 'adequacy'.) Great realists all share the ability to penetrate the great social problems of their day and to reveal their underlying reality. They do this through characters who, once conceived by their creator, proceed to take on an independent life of their own. This is where Zola is alleged to be so deficient, in his inability to create such memorable types. Balzac, even when he is creating the 'novel of disillusionment' in *Lost Illusions*, always succeeds in giving us characters who exist both as individuals and as types, who exhibit both personal and class traits, and he deploys characterisation as a means of pointing up the differences that can exist between individuals even of the same social type. All capitalists are not the same; they respond in a variety of ways to changing, often highly confusing and disorienting, social circumstances. Balzac's characters come alive as individuals grappling with the complexities of capitalist development in early to mid-nineteenth-century French society. Zola, on the other hand, blurs the differences between his characters. His 'scientific' naturalistic method 'always seeks the average . . . this grey statistical mean, the point at which all internal contradictions are blunted, where the great and the petty, the noble and the base, the beautiful and the ugly are all mediocre "products" together' (p. 91). Such standardisation, a world away from the richness and diversity of human behaviour found in Balzac's novels, sounds the death-knell of great literature for Lukács, and means that, unlike Balzac or Dickens, Zola fails to create those highly desirable memorable types: 'Zola, although his life-work is very extensive, has never created a single character who grew to be a type, a by-word, almost a living being' (p. 93). One might object that this is a very limiting criterion for success as a novelist, and, even if it were to be accepted, at best a rather subjective one. One reader's living being may be dead on the page to another – 'living', like 'real' or 'adequate', is a slippery term, which raises more questions than it ever manages to answer. A similar problem arises when Lukács remarks that 'realism means a three-dimensionality, an all-roundness that endows with independent life characters and human relationships' (p. 6) in that agreement as to how three-dimensionality, etc. are to be recognised would be hard to come by.

Naturalism invariably comes off badly when compared to realism in *SER*, and it is worth dwelling on their perceived differences for a moment. Realism gives us memorable types, living beings with an air of independent existence, and a clear sense of the economic forces at work in society at any one point in history. In Marxist terms we could say that realism reveals a society's infrastructure such that we can observe the effect it has on individual behaviour at superstructural level: social beings are seen to be the basis of social consciousness. Naturalism, on the other hand, obscures the reader's view of the infrastructure and presents us with diminished individual human beings who are dwarfed by the large-scale social forces that confront them. Those forces are impersonal and implacable, leaving little room for manoeuvre at the individual level. What is missing in naturalism for Lukács is any sense of the dialectical interaction of individual and social forces which is such a prominent feature of the best realist writing. One might say that Zola's naturalism is almost too successful in showing how the capitalist system crushes individuals. His heart may be in the right place, and it is clear that his sympathies lie with the downtrodden, but what we are left with after reading Zola is an awareness of just how powerless we are as individuals in the face of an all-conquering capitalism. The system is in control, and it is hard to see how mere individuals can combat it in any meaningful way. As Lukács' pupil István Mészaros put it, it is not so much nature that naturalists are depicting in their 'tediously detailed "faithful" manner' as dehumanised nature.[3]

Zola's naturalism prefigures the landscape of modernism, where alienated, isolated individuals are pictured as being at the mercy of vast impersonal forces which control their fate. It is this landscape that Lukács will proceed to be so critical of in *MCR*. What he describes as 'the grey average of naturalism' tends to dominate in Zola's narratives, where we are vouchsafed only the 'outward trappings of modern life' (p. 92). When Zola does manage to transcend this grey average it is merely to lapse into the picturesque romanticism of Victor Hugo, an author who is dismissed for the sin of 'bombastic monumentalism' (p. 93). It is the monotony rather than the richness, diversity and sheer dynamism of capitalist life that Zola shows us – for that dynamism we must turn to authors such as Balzac. In the final analysis Zola proves to be one of that considerable body of writers whom capitalism prevents from fulfilling their talent: for all his political correctness ultimately a victim of the very system that he set out to disparage in his fiction. The clear suggestion is that naturalism fails to further the class struggle and that it may even impede the development of the appropriate kind of consciousness for that struggle.

Flaubert is another author to be compared unfavourably with Balzac, and in fact for Lukács the revision of nineteenth-century European literary history can be reduced to a starkly simple opposition: 'which of the two, Balzac or Flaubert, was the greatest novelist, the typical classic of the 19th century?' (p. 2). This is a classic Lukácsian ploy to be duplicated in several other studies, but, as he emphasises, it is no mere matter of taste that is at stake, but the novel's entire significance as a sociological and ideological phenomenon. Flaubert, a consistent practitioner of the 'novel of disillusionment', is accused by Lukács of communicating a sense of frustration, pessimism and even nihilism, which can only render his criticism of bourgeois life counter-productive. Flaubert's theory of impartiality (*impassibilité*), like Zola's naturalism, reduces

the author to the status of a mere observer whose eye for detail
effectively represents a cul-de-sac for the development of realism.
So narrow is Flaubert's art, especially when compared to Balzac's,
that it can tell us nothing much of note about society at large:
Flaubert's creations rarely attain the status of types from whom
significant lessons can be learned. The author as detached and
socially alienated observer is a typical outcome for literature after
1848, with Lukács suggesting a connection between the collapse of
the revolutionary ideals of that momentous year and authorial
world-views and methods. The Flaubert who confides to a friend
in a letter of 1850 that 'We have a many-voiced orchestra, a rich
palette, varied sources of power. As for tricks and devices, we have
more of those than ever. But we lack inner life, the soul of things,
the idea of the writer's subject' (quoted, p. 42) is, in his bitterness
and tone of despair, the authentic voice of the new, diminished
realism that follows in the wake of 1848 when, Lukács argues, the
way that bourgeois society proceeded to develop destroyed the
conditions that had made great realism possible. It is against this
bleak backdrop of revolutionary failure and a renewed spirit of
political reaction in European society that post-Balzacian authors,
however unfairly, are going to be judged by Lukács. Those who,
like Tolstoy, contrive to reassert the virtues of the older realism in
such unpromising circumstances, who do not fall prey to the lure
of the 'novel of disillusionment', are to be doubly praised.

Lukács notes three main negative traits of Western European
realism post-1848 which differentiate it from the practice of the
great realists of the previous generation. In the first place the sheer
breadth of vision of the older realism disappears; second, the economic roots of social relationships are obscured: third, an excess of
detail replaces the art of the selection of 'typical' or essential detail.
The overall result is to transform the author from involved participant to passive observer of social life, and it is this passivity, in
effect the difference between the authorial practice of a Flaubert
and a Balzac, that points the way to the ideologically insidious
world of modernism, and therefore draws Lukács' disapproval.
The ground is being prepared for the critique of modernism that
was to bring Lukács such notoriety.

Tolstoy is one of those authors who manages to keep 'great
realism' alive in the aftermath of the 1848 débâcle, and he is in
consequence one of Lukács' enduring heroes who figures promi-

nently throughout his critical writings. Again in Tolstoy we note that distinctive hallmark of great realism, the discrepancy between intention and performance, between political prejudices and the comprehensive, correct and objective depiction of social reality: 'Tolstoy had of course no conception of the true nature of the Russian revolution. But being a writer of genius, he faithfully recorded certain essential traits of reality and thus, without his knowledge, and contrary to his conscious intentions, he became the poetic mirror of certain aspects of the revolutionary development in Russia' (p. 137). Tolstoy manages to present life in the Russia of his day with great fidelity, despite his aristocratic background, and the ability to transcend the limitations of one's class in this way, as well as the refusal to succumb to the pessimism and nihilism that overcame artists such as Flaubert, declare Tolstoy to be the true heir of the great realist tradition, which, it is argued, passes out of France and England into Russia and Scandinavia in the post-1848 era. Lukács notes a closer connection between literature and life in Russia than in the West, and Tolstoy is treated as very much representative of this closeness.

In Tolstoy there is a breadth of vision to rival, perhaps even surpass, Balzac, and the realisation, so important to success in the realist mode of writing, that 'everything is linked up with everything else' (p. 145). On this score Tolstoy, his aristocratic and landowning background notwithstanding, becomes the poet of that peasant revolt in Russian life which lasts from 1861 to 1905. As an example of this talent Lukács cites the description of Prince Nekhlyudov's regimental life in Tolstoy's late novel *Resurrection*, where the details of the prince's uniform (made, cleaned and put into his hands by others, as Tolstoy points out) are designed 'to stress the social implications which determine the use of such objects' rather than simply piling them up for their own sake as would be the case in naturalistic narrative method, and, as Lukács observes approvingly, those 'social implications point to exploitation, the exploitation of the peasants by the landowners' (p. 146). This is the selective use of detail to bring out essential truths about the character and his society that Lukács regards as one of the greatest strengths of realist writing.

It should not be thought that great realism provides the answers to the social problems that tax Marxist critics. Tolstoy, as Lukács reminds us here and elsewhere, in the main proffers incorrect and reactionary answers to the problem of how to overcome the exploitation identified above; what we are to appreciate in Tolstoy Lukács suggests, in what is one of the great insights of his criticism, is 'the putting of the question and not the answer given to it' (p. 146). This observation, drawn from some comments Chekhov made about Tolstoy, brings out the fundamental difference between Lukács' brand of Marxist analysis and that of the 'vulgar sociologists' or socialist realists, for both of whom the correct *answer* was of paramount importance. Lukács' concentration on 'the question' opens up literary history to the enquiring materialist mind rather than reducing aesthetics, as so often happens in the 'vulgar Marxist' approach, to a series of relatively facile judgements based on an author's political affiliation. The mere fact of being bourgeois does not disqualify an author from being useful to the socialist cause in Lukács' view, and it is this open-mindedness – so radical, one must repeat, in the context of 1930s Moscow – that keeps Lukács' critical writings alive for later generations unlikely to be persuaded by the black-and-white certainties of the socialist realists. Lukács can be as harsh as any capitalist critic about the failings of what he calls 'publicistic criticism', that ' "purely" social or political attitude to literature, which judges past and present according to the superficial slogans of the day, without considering the real artistic content of the work in question, or caring whether it is a great work of art or a piece of worthless trash' (p. 125). It is one of his abiding virtues as a critic that he never allows himself to decline into a mere propagandist in this way.

Socialist realism can have its good points, however, and Lukács is quick to acknowledge this in the case of Gorki, described as the first great socialist realist. Gorki is held to be particularly successful in showing us the social forces which shape the destiny of individuals, and also in refusing to succumb to that withdrawal from life so characteristic of modern authors, whose fictions soon decline as a result into empty and lifeless abstractions. Gorki's characters are consistently confronted by all the key economic and political factors which determine individual fate in a capitalist society. In consequence he points the way forward for the realist tradition, becoming, in Lukács' approving words, 'the socialist revolution's greatest literary tribune'.[4] The realist tradition is, therefore, not just an historical curiosity, but a living organism, which can grow and adapt itself to society's changing needs. Lukács sets himself the task in this period of fostering that tradition in a climate fairly hostile to the claims of bourgeois novelists, and he will remain a self-appointed guardian of great realism.

Realism is a term over which much critical ink has been spilled and we might now consider whether Lukács leaves us any the wiser after *SER* about its character. We have seen how much stress Lukács places on characterisation in his exposition of the concerns of realism ('the central aesthetic problem'), and what he thinks realist characterisation should involve – three-dimensionality, all-roundedness, independent life, memorability. We have also seen what he considers to be the main injunction laid on the realist author, that he 'must honestly record, without fear or favour, everything he sees around him' (p. 138). We know too that realism need not mean adhering to socialist principles: discrepancy between intention and performance is no bar to entering the great realist pantheon; it may in fact be a point in your favour as it seems to be with Balzac and Tolstoy. Yet it is a moot point whether any of this brings us significantly closer to understanding what realism actually is, or why it is deemed to be so preferable to other literary styles. Three-dimensionality, all-roundedness, independence of existence and memorability are all in the eye of the beholder it could be argued, and one wonders just how easy it would be to come to general agreement as to their presence in any given novel. In what precise sense is a Balzac character more rounded and independent than a Zola creation? The answer is by no means obvious. And what does it really mean to be rounded and independent in a literary context? Literary characters are constructs, realist ones no less so than naturalist or anti-realist ones. Lukács can often give the impression of losing sight of literature's constructed, *artificial* nature – a realisation that modernists were putting to such devastating effect in their productions, where time-honoured assumptions were being subjected to ruthless, and revolutionary, challenge. Even for the 1930s and 1940s, so much closer to the realist tradition than we are now, Lukács can seem quite old-fashioned – one is tempted to say quite *literal* – in his view of how literature and literary characters, as well as the reading *process*, function. As for memorability, that is surely the weakest of all the criteria Lukács advances: one person's memorable literary character is another's boring cliché – and just think how memorability can fluctuate from generation to generation. Little Nell was initially memorable, later quite laughable (the latter is a kind of memorability, of course, but not what Lukács had in mind, one suspects).

Similar problems arise with the idea of authors honestly recording everything that they see around them. No doubt all authors feel that they are doing just this – Flaubert and Zola no less than Balzac and Tolstoy – and since Lukács argues that much of what an author reveals about the society around him is *unintentional* it is hard to see what 'honestly' means in this context anyway. Neither can any author reveal 'everything' – the author has to be selective, as Lukács concedes. In fact, the ability to select the 'typical' or 'essential' out of the background of 'everything' is what distinguishes the great realist in Lukács' scheme of things; but naturalists are no less selective in their way; they simply give the audience more selectively chosen detail, which prompts the question: 'At what point do we pass from the essential to the excessive?' Lukács provides little real guidance (in truth, it is hard to see how he could), relying instead on examples of passages drawn from approved authors – Tolstoy, Gorki, Balzac, Stendhal. How one *generalises* from these examples is, however, where the problems begin.

As for the discrepancy between intention and performance, it is problematic to be praising authors for something they are doing unintentionally. This is a criticism often levelled against the 'reading against the grain' school – that it concentrates on the unwitting at the expense of the witting – and in his prefiguring of that critical method, Lukács is just as open to attack. We are thrown back on the notion that some authors are recording more honestly than others, but since the precise nature of the relationship between honesty and selectivity is, as we have discovered, difficult, if not impossible, to determine, we are left none the wiser. Lukács' conception of realism is, as Rodney Livingstone has argued in his introduction to *ER*, a form of essentialism, and, like most forms of essentialism, full of unexamined assumptions that can be probed away at by the sceptic. Lukácsian realism is, in fact, ripe for deconstruction in its preference for loaded binary oppositions. But to put the positive case for it, I will turn back to Rodney Livingstone who claims:

Realism is then not a substitute for political action: it is the structure of consciousness that accompanies it. It is this that constitutes the strength of Lukács' position. . . . Realism may serve, as Brecht thought, as a cultural prop of the ruling classes, but this is no ineluctable fate. Lukács has done more than anyone, perhaps, to demonstrate its 'progressive' potential. (*ER*, Intro., p. 21)

Caught between a Stalinist-inspired socialist realism asking for propaganda on the one side, and an iconoclastic modernism throwing out the baby with the bathwater on the other, Lukács' assertion of the progressive potential of the bourgeois realist tradition is no mean achievement, and from a postmodern perspective one of the most perceptive aspects of his critical writing. Lukács is always concerned, as are many postmodernist theorists, with keeping up a real dialogue with the past (we shall be returning to the postmodernist implications of such dialogue in chapter 8), and that is one of his great strengths as a critic and cultural theorist.

The Historical Novel

HN covers a very broad canvas and is in many ways the most successful of Lukács' critical studies. This survey of the historical novel in Europe ranges from Sir Walter Scott in the early nineteenth century through to the anti-fascist humanists of the 1930s when Lukács was writing (the book was composed in Moscow in 1936–7 and published in Russian shortly afterwards). Although the study is not an exhaustive one, Lukács selecting authors and works who are most representative from his theoretical standpoint, it still traverses a great deal of ground to realise its rather Hegelian-sounding objective. 'What I had in mind', Lukács recalls in his preface to a later edition (1960), 'was a theoretical examination of the interaction between the historical spirit and the great genres of literature which portray the totality of history.'[5] One significant omission is the historical novel in Soviet literature, which Lukács regrets he cannot deal with owing to a lack of translations at the time. Lukács regards the modern historical novel (from Scott onwards) as a product of specific historical forces – the Enlightenment, the French Revolution, the revolutionary wars and the rise and fall of Napoleon in particular – which transformed history into a pan-European, mass experience. The outcome of these momentous events was that Europeans came to see their lives as historically conditioned, a point Hegel was also to make with reference to nations in his philosophical works. Hegel was much influenced by this new sense of historicism in European society, which conceived of man as a product of his own activity in history, and came to regard the total life of humanity as one vast historical process. This new historical consciousness informs all Scott's novels too, and Lukács draws parallels between the respective projects of Hegel and Scott without wishing to suggest anything remotely resembling direct influence. What is clear is that in his own individual way each author has absorbed the new historical consciousness and made it the basis of both his world-view and his writing.

Lukács' work on Scott represents one of his finest efforts as a critic. In an era when Scott is more admired than studied, Lukács' masterly analysis of his *oeuvre* reminds us of the scale of Scott's achievement.[6] For Lukács, Scott is an author with a deeper grasp of historical necessity than any other before him, and he provides some persuasive arguments, both here and elsewhere, to support his claim that Scott is the founder of the classical historical novel. Scott is approached as a great realist worthy to be included in the company of Balzac and Tolstoy, and like those figures a great writer despite his social and political views – there is the same discrepancy between intention and performance to be noted in Scott's work as in that of his continental counterparts. Scott is undeniably a conservative, but his keen sense of historical process makes him one of the most representative writers of his age, with a particular talent for creating what Lukács calls 'historical-social' types to exemplify historical change. Characterisation once again holds the key to novelistic success. Scott's heroes are typical of their age in being caught up in complex historical processes of which they are often only dimly aware – the death of feudalism in Scottish clan life, for example – and, one might also say, for their sheer ordinariness. They are not larger-than-life supermen, but normal mortals grappling with historical forces at the level of daily life. It is the historical process itself which is the real hero in Scott, which can lead him to be quite cavalier on occasion with his main characters – Waverley and Quentin Durward disappear from the pages of their eponymous novels for long stretches, and indeed the latter is little more than a cipher in his narrative's closing stages. Process and historical change would seem to be what fired Scott's imagination, and the deliberate underplaying of the roles of his lead characters prevents our attention from being deflected by the main business at hand. The fact that Quentin Durward is a marginal figure at the end of his own tale is unimportant: what *is* important is that we see in the conclusion of the narrative the triumph of the modern state over the chaos of feudalism. It is not hard to understand why Lukács, that most Hegelian and historically conscious of Marxist critics, would be so attracted by Scott's narrative method despite the highly conservative politics underpinning it: it is the attraction of one dialectical thinker to another.

It is this strongly dialectical historical consciousness that distinguishes Scott from previous practitioners of the historical novel, none of whom is considered to share his talent for bringing out the interaction between individual behaviour and historical process. The great transformations of history are traced down to their impact on popular life in Scott. Thus we can observe the Jacobite rebellions in Scotland through the eyes of a wide range of characters over several novels in such a way as to reveal the confused socio-political situation from which they sprung, rather than having it presented to us as a conflict between an elite of great men. Scott is particularly adept at rendering the confusion of historical crisis, and captures with great acuteness the atmosphere of shifting allegiance, ambiguity of motive and mingling of public and private interest – in a word, the dialectics of such crises.

Waverley and *Rob Roy* are classic examples of Scott's abilities in this regard with their leading figures (Edward Waverley and Francis Osbaldistone, respectively) running the gamut of human emotions in response to the Jacobite rebellions unfolding rapidly and chaotically around them. In such cases Scott's conservatism proves no barrier to honest recording of the tumultuous state of Scottish society at the time, nor to the historical necessities ceaselessly at work beneath that society's surface. In his Jacobite novels Scott succeeds in showing us the 'unequalled human greatness of this primitive order [the Scottish clan system] as well as the inner necessity of its tragic downfall' (p. 61). Whatever the poetry of his portrayal of Scottish clan life (and Lukács feels this to be considerable), Scott never shies away from acknowledging the necessity of its decline in the face of changing socio-political circumstances. In this sense he is, as Lukács assertively argues, no Romantic: invariably, he puts the right question, regardless of what his political prejudices would appear to dictate.

The historical-social type at the centre of Scott's novels, there-fore, serves in his very ordinariness and lack of superheroic qualities to focus our attention on the real business of Scott's project – historical process seen at points of particular crisis. It is the role of such types to act as catalysts for the process in question: 'to bring the extremes whose struggle fills the novel, whose clash expresses artistically a great crisis in society, into contact with one another' (p. 36). Scott's protagonists are given just enough indi-viduality to make their fates of interest to us as readers, not enough to make them appear to be radically different from their fellows or immune to the problems of historical change. The typical Scott hero, Lukács observes, is 'a more or less mediocre, average English gentleman' who 'possesses a certain, though never outstanding, degree of practical intelligence, a certain moral fortitude and de-cency which even rises to a capacity for self-sacrifice, but which never grows into a sweeping human passion, is never the enrap-tured devotion to a great cause' (p. 32). We have the breadth of vision, the sense of the underlying roots of social relationships, and the selectively typical detail in the treatment of these characters' fates within a changing social order, that to Lukács signals great realism. In sum, Scott is a prime example of what great realism can achieve in the pre-1848 period, one of the fountainheads of the classical form of the historical novel where historical process is made to come alive through the unfolding of the fates of the main characters.

Lukács finds a particular parallel between Scott and Hegel in the way that the former approaches the larger-than-life figures in his novels, that is, the leaders of clans, movements, rebellions, etc. (Vich Ian Vohr in *Waverley*, or Burley in *Old Mortality*, for ex-ample). These 'world-historical' figures emerge naturally out of the character of the times in Scott and are never isolated or ahistorical in nature (as Carlyle's heroes, in contrast, generally are). Such an individual in Hegel arises too 'upon the broad basis of the world of "maintaining individuals"' (Hegel's term for men in civil society) (p. 40). Scott's realism triumphs, whatever the character being pictured, because of his sure grasp of this world of 'maintaining individuals', hence the fascination he holds for a critic like Lukács, who finds similar qualities in Fennimore Cooper, possibly the only worthy follower of Scott in the English language.

Rather surprisingly perhaps, given the contemporaneity of his material, Balzac features in this survey of the historical novel. What Balzac offers his audience in the *Comédie Humaine* is, Lukács argues, 'the *present as history*' (p. 94). Balzac's treatment of the period 1789–1848 over the course of the *Comédie Humaine* brings to mind Scott in its keen sense of process, change and necessity: it represents the 'extension of the historical novel into an historical picture of the present' (p. 96). We have already seen the virtues that Balzac's work holds for Lukács, so they will not be rehearsed again, but it is interesting to note that Lukács feels the need to place these virtues within the context of the historical novel as if in its classical form it constituted a model for novelistic practice pre-1848. Post-1848 things are to take a different turn, as Lukács proceeds to demonstrate.

1848 is once again regarded as a watershed in European social and cultural history, a year in which 'for the first time the proletariat enters upon the world-historical stage as an armed mass, resolved upon the final struggle' (p. 202). While concerned to ensure that the links between the general socio-political tendencies of the period and issues of literary form are not conceived of too straight-forwardly, Lukács nevertheless identifies significant changes in au-thorial practice and attitude in the aftermath of 1848, one of which is the historical novel's loss of popular character. In general he observes a turning away from the notion of historical process on the part of bourgeois authors (Flaubert being a notable example). The splitting of Europe into 'two nations' (the immediate impetus for the development of 'the industrial novel' in England), which 1848 put the seal on, meant that authors became progressively more alienated from the social totality and their perspective restricted to one or other of those 'two nations'. The breadth of a Scott or a Balzac is increasingly difficult to achieve in this new cultural climate and it effectively spells the end of the classical historical novel. In Lukács' emotive words, post-1848 'everything human is submerged under the desert sands of capitalist prose' (p. 244). The historical novel henceforth declines into the presentation of a series of episodes, which negates the idea of progress and change which lay at the heart of Scott and Balzac's projects.

This turning inward, this retreat from public to private con-cerns that is so characteristic of the literature of the period, is to Lukács an ideologically regressive gesture and few authors show

themselves capable of resisting its lure. What this regressive gesture means for the historical novel is demonstrated through a
series of analyses of later nineteenth-century authors, not all of
them very well known in the English-speaking world, such as the
team of Emile Erckmann and Alexandre Chatrian, Charles de
Coster and Conrad Frederick Meyer. The latter is taken to be the
most representative of historical novelists in this period and it is
worth dwelling on his case to see what the decline of realism in the
context of the historical novel is felt to involve. Meyer (1825–98)
was a Swiss novelist with a predilection for Renaissance themes,
who, in common with much of the German middle class
post-1848, was caught up in the wave of adulation for the Prussian
statesman and voice of German unity, Bismarck. The Bismarckian
character, authoritarian, dictatorial, apparently superhuman, begins to infiltrate Meyer's historical novels, which generally take as
their focus enigmatic, lonely hero or genius figures, whose destiny
is to decide the course of nations and history. Thus in *The Tempta-
tion of Pescara*, Pescara himself is left to decide in lone speculation
whether Italy is to be liberated from foreign domination, and in
cavalier fashion concludes it is not. Where Scott presents us with
world-historical figures Meyer gives us great men with self-
appointed missions, and power as an abstract force. Individuals
like Pescara are fundamentally unknowable and hint at the possibility that history itself is too – something beyond the grasp of
the common man or woman, the preserve of the superhuman hero
or genius. The inner conflicts of Meyer's heroes 'do not grow out
of the real historical conditions of the given period, out of the
popular life of the period. Instead they are specifically modern
conflicts of passion and conscience in an individual artificially
isolated by capitalist life' (p. 269). The novel of historical process
declines in Meyer into the novel of psychological drama – and
even more significantly, into the psychological drama of the isolated individual. Great realism is but a fading memory at such
moments. Not everyone succumbs to this powerful cultural tendency to turn inward (Lukács is careful to observe that an historical
trend can be general without being exclusive), but it is a difficult
cycle to break out of and one that is indicative of the bourgeoisie's
growing control of social consciousness. Even a writer of Dickens'
stature cannot prevent psychological drama from marring his ex-
cursion into history in *A Tale of Two Cities*.

Lukács follows the historical novel through into modern times, the age of democratic humanism, with a concern, not all that common in the socialist realist camp, to be as fair to his subjects as possible. Although he can be harshly judgemental, as when he refers to Victor Hugo's 'bombastic monumentalism' and Flaubert's 'decorative archaeologism' (p. 301), Lukács is committed to communicating the complexity of the historical process and the writer's relation to it. 'Every writer is the son of his age', he remarks in standard enough Marxist sociological fashion, but then points out that 'the contradictory tendencies of the age – the decay of the imperialist period and the democratic protest of the working masses, literary decadence and the yearning for popular roots – affect the writer in a contradictory and criss-cross fashion' (p. 305). It is not the least of Lukács' virtues as a critic that, in an age and a social context that favoured propaganda, he was so willing to pursue these contradictory and criss-cross currents in the work of bourgeois authors. One is struck even now by the honesty and thoroughness Lukács brings to his task (as he remarked in a letter to a friend, Anna Seghers, 'believe me, dear Anna, I never pass judgement on a writer before I have studied him very thoroughly' (*ER*, p. 184)), and it cannot be repeated enough that these are by no means standard elements in Marxist cultural analyses of the 1930s, either inside or outside the Soviet Union. Engineering of human souls was not necessarily synonymous with painstaking critique.

Lukács' focus in the concluding stages of *HN* is on the historical novel of militant, anti-fascist humanism and there are some particularly penetrating analyses of the novels of, among others, Heinrich Mann. Distressed as he is by the growth of Hitlerian fascism, Lukács sees it as providing the basis for an oppositional humanism, which will inaugurate a new era in German national life and literature. It is against this background of opposition to fascism that Lukács proceeds to analyse a group of mainly German historical novels. Heinrich Mann is considered to be in the forefront of this developing tradition, and an excellent example of an author who has managed to break with the tendency of the bourgeois historical novel (Flaubert, Meyer, etc.) to render history private, to transform it into a tale based on an eccentric individual psychology. Mann's novel *Henri IV* is singled out for special praise. Here we have a work vividly portraying a critical turning-point in the history of the French nation (St Bartholomew's night), which also succeeds in presenting its protagonist with a high degree of realistically observed psychological complexity. Yet the contradictory and criss-cross currents of Mann's time leave their mark upon a work which, in Lukács' view, ultimately is, for all its admirable qualities, seriously flawed. The problem lies in the narrative method chosen – biography. Biography, identified by Lukács as one of the most important tendencies in the modern historical novel, prevents an author like Mann from aspiring to the breadth of a Scott or a Balzac, because the attitude informing the biographical form is one that conceives of history as the province of great men. No matter how sensitively handled – and Lukács freely acknowledges Mann's sensitivity as a writer – biography represents a dilution of the theme of historical process and of the world-historical quality of a fictional character. The effect of biography is to diminish the novel's subsidiary characters, who 'lose their individual concrete and complex dialectics [to] become planets revolving around the sun of the biography's hero' (p. 387). When this happens it is no longer putting the right question to its society.

Biography is not enough, therefore, to recreate an historical period in all its complexity. Even its greatest exponents – and Lukács makes it clear that Mann is in that category – will fall far short of Scott's achievement. 'Reality as a whole', Lukács points out, 'is always richer and more varied than even the richest work of art' (p. 365), but even richer than a work that chooses to remain at the biographical level. Lukács is not so much concerned to condemn Mann – he declares *Henri IV* to be an important work and Mann a writer of special significance in the fight against fascism – as to register the limitations that the biographical method can impose on even the most talented and well-intentioned of authors in the anti-fascist camp. 'The facts of a great man's life', Lukács insists in his most unequivocal manner, 'tell us at best the particular occasion on which something great was achieved, but they never give us the real context, the real chain of causation as a result of which this great accomplishment played its great part in history' (p. 369). What those facts cannot do in any really systematic fashion is convey a feeling of historical necessity, and it is this phenomenon which Lukács insists must be found at the heart of the historical novel. The driving forces of history, which Scott was

so able at revealing, recede into the background when the biographical element begins to dominate, much to the detriment of
the historical novel's socio-political usefulness.

Scott can probably be regarded as the real hero of *HN*, the
author who keeps historical process in the foreground, who never
fails to acknowledge historical necessity, who never allows his
narratives to decline into mere biography nor indulges in exoticism
for its own sake. The classical historical novel becomes a standard
by which all later products will be judged, although Lukács is
scrupulously careful in keeping us aware of the complex sociological imperatives that lie behind all decisions about narrative
method. Mann and his contemporaries are not simply dismissed
out of hand, but instead painstakingly analysed in terms of the
cultural situation in which they find themselves. Lukács genuinely
wants to determine just what is of value in their novels at a time of
full-scale historical crisis, in the light of the socialist consciousness
that he brings to bear on them. What that consciousness is constantly striving to do is to establish the link between ideology and
literature: 'Precisely the development of the historical novel shows
most clearly how what appear to be purely formal, compositional
problems – e.g., whether the great figures of history should be
principal heroes or minor figures – so obviously conceal ideological
and political problems of the highest importance' (pp. 401–2). It is
because literature is so bound up with the ideology of its time that
it must be examined critically by Marxists, whose duty, as Lukács
sees it, is not just to explain the impoverishment of so much of
modern literature but to measure it 'against the highest demands
of the artistic reflection of historical reality' (p. 403) and to pronounce it lacking in no uncertain terms.

Underlying Lukács' enquiry is the belief that literature is one of
the primary means of forming social attitudes such that it matters
whether great men are lionised or not, whether they are seen to be
self-created or products of historical process and historical necessity. Lukács was writing, after all, at a time when the perils of
allowing great men to dominate history were only too obvious –
Hitler being the outstanding example in the 1930s but with Stalin,
as Lukács was beginning to realise to his cost, not all that far
behind in terms of the dangers posed to society at large. The
history of the historical novel becomes a key to the kind of society
that Lukács is living in, and what it tells him is that we need more

world-historical and 'maintaining' individuals and fewer heroes or tortured geniuses. What can be said in favour of an author like Heinrich Mann is that he has taken a step in the right direction in comparison to the previous generation of historical novelists, or to most of his peers for that matter, and for that he deserves praise even if Lukács still feels that, in general, the anti-fascist humanists tend to take the path of least resistance in their fiction and to evade the real question facing a writer in any era – 'the question of the historical genesis of the present' (p. 414). What the time requires is a renewal of the historical novel, and by renewal Lukács does not mean a revival of the classical form as practised by Scott, but 'a renewal in the form of a negation of a negation' (p. 423); that is to say, a Hegelian 'sublation', a raising of the historical novel to new heights by an overcoming and dissolution of the contradictions of the old. In that way the historical novel, whose new form Lukács can only guess at, will contribute to the destruction of the many harmful legacies of the bourgeois past which still abound in present-day society.

Many of the criticisms that were made of *SER*'s essays can also be made of *HN*. Realism is once again assumed to be the correct style for authors to adopt and we find characterisation being praised for its 'typicality' in a way that recalls the 'memorable types' criterion of *SER*. Great store is laid by 'honest recording'. But this raises the same problems as before about intentionality and selectivity: are we praising authors for unintended features of their works? In what way is one selection of details from the world around us *necessarily* more 'typical' than another? One might also query the weight being put on the year 1848 in both these literary-historical surveys. 1848 is a year of immense significance to Marxists, but one wonders whether it casts quite as much of a cultural shadow as Lukács claims. History is rarely that clear-cut, and it is difficult to determine the impact of given historical events on given individuals, even in the mass. Above all we have the problem of Lukács' essentialism, the view that there is an essence to a literary text which we can grasp in its entirety and apply in an uncritical manner to social or political problems. This is no longer a view likely to go unquestioned, although to be fair to Lukács it is not a sin even late twentieth-century Marxists can be said to be entirely free of, as we shall see when we consider his critical legacy in the work of Fredric Jameson. Perhaps we can return to Rodney

Livingstone's remarks about realism and suggest that it is enough for Lukács to have demonstrated that there is progressive potential in the historical novel, a form which was beginning to look distinctly creaky by the 1930s. It is also noteworthy, as it was in the case of *SER*, how skilfully Lukács contrives to position himself between a propaganda-conscious socialist realism and an iconoclastic modernism. From what looks at first sight to be distinctly unpromising material, Lukács manages to fashion one of the classic studies of the relationship between literature and ideology in *HN* and to make it seem highly relevant to the contemporary socio-political situation of the struggle against fascism – a considerable triumph by almost any critical reckoning.

Essays on Realism

ER is a collection of essays written in the 1930s and it takes the battle for realism into areas such as the modern German proletarian novel and the expressionist movement. Its concluding essay 'Tribune or Bureaucrat?' (published in 1940 and claimed by Lukács to be a veiled attack on the personality cult of Stalin) will be dealt with in chapter 7. Our interest here lies in Lukács' attacks on experimental literature and also in his fascinating correspondence with Anna Seghers, whose close friendship with Lukács does not prevent her from asking some awkward questions about Lukács' conception of realism – questions which Lukács never satisfactorily answers.

Ernst Ottwalt's novel *Denn sie wissen, was sie tun (For They Know Not What They Do)* is made to bear the brunt of Lukács' considerable dislike of the reportage style of modernist writing (also seen in the work of such writers as Upton Sinclair and John Dos Passos). Ottwalt, a member of the German Communist Party and the League of Proletarian Writers, makes extensive use of journalistic techniques in *Denn sie wissen*, an exposure of the justice system in the Weimar Republic, and although on the face of it this sounds like the kind of sublation of the historical novel that Lukács is seeking in this period of his career he is nevertheless moved to condemn the reportage style as a mere experiment in form. *Denn sie wissen*'s speeches and reports lifted from actual court cases cannot in Lukács' view replace 'portrayal', and he is adamant that

the novel requires a different form of characterisation from a journalistic report. The argument is very similar to the one mounted
against naturalism: reportage is not selective enough in its presentation of characters or events, nor does it achieve typicality; in
Lukács' later aesthetic terms of reference, the style excludes itself
from the category of specialty. We are not drawn into the lives of
the characters, who hardly exist as real beings in the pages of the
narrative. A telling comparison is made between Ottwalt and
Tolstoy. When Tolstoy tackles a similar theme to *Denn sie wissen*
in *Resurrection* he ensures that the reader is given a comprehensive
picture of the Russian judicial system which includes the perspectives of both those inside and those outside the system. In the
process we become deeply involved in the lives of the characters
affected by the system as Tolstoy does everything he can to inspire
his readers to take a keen interest in the characters' fates. In
Ottwalt, on the other hand, all we receive is a series of dry reports
detailing the workings of the system, its arbitrary character and
class-biased nature, where the author 'only speaks about these
things, he never gives us the things themselves' (p. 570). What is
missing is *portrayal*, precisely what the great realists are so skilled
at. Without portrayal, Lukács contends, there can be no pretence
of realism nor of its acute sensitivity to historical process, necessity
and change.

While Ottwalt might seem to be attempting to find a new way of
rendering the present as history, Lukács' intense dislike of experimentation denies the possibility of this avowedly proletarian
author being viewed in a positive, socialism enhancing way. Expressionism too is rejected for its experimental quality, and here
Lukács insists on some very concrete connections between literature and ideology, with expressionism being condemned as simply
one of the several tendencies in bourgeois ideology that eventually
develop into fascism. Expressionism is to be seen as an extreme
case of the bourgeois tendency, so prevalent in the post-1848
historical novel, to evade the really important problems of the day,
being for Lukács no more than attacks on symptoms rather than
causes. Lukács is particularly critical of the movement's subjectiv-
ism, which he considers is so extreme as to border on solipsism.
There is a lack, in other words, of typicality or world-historicality
in the expressionist style, and Lukács will invariably be critical of
any literature which shies away from comprehensiveness of vision,

as we saw with his treatment of the biographical approach to the historical novel. Not even the Nazis' later rejection of expressionism as decadent can alter Lukács' belief in the historical correctness of his analysis.

Lukács' correspondence with Anna Seghers, on the eve of the outbreak of the Second World War, provides some fascinating debate about the nature of realism and is still worth attention. Seghers claims that there is no fundamental disagreement between them on the issue of realism, but is soon taxing Lukács with a lack of conceptual rigour:

> Please again define exactly what you understand by realism. This request is not superfluous. In your discussions, you use terminology in different ways, and often without precision. It is ambiguous, for example, whether you mean the realism of *today*, or realism *in general*, i.e. an orientation to the highest possible reality attainable at a particular time. (p. 171)

The criticism is a good one in foregrounding the relativity (not to mention the slipperiness) of the term, a relativity which Lukács' essentialism will not allow him to see. Seghers goes on to relativise further the term when she suggests that all art is realistic in its own particular way: 'I should like to ask in return whether there is any authentic work of art which does not contain a substance of realism, i.e. a tendency towards bringing reality into our consciousness' (p. 173). Lukács' notion of a fixed concept of realism holding over time begins to dissolve under such an analysis (although one might query how 'authentic' is going to be defined), and this opens the way for modernism to be brought into the Marxist aesthetic canon as realistic for its day, age and cultural situation. Lukács is not convinced; and while conceding that elements of realism can be found even in anti-realist works, still holds to the idea of there being objective standards ('realism in general') by which we can determine whether a given work has achieved the highest possible reality available to it at a particular time. In the absence of such objective standards Lukács claims, revealing an unfortunately ethnocentrist side to his character, we would be in danger of succumbing to 'the narrowness of that "avant-gardism" which puts Negro sculpture and the drawings of the insane on the same level as Phidias and Rembrandt, even preferring them where possible' (p. 182). Realism remains the gatekeeper for Marxist aesthetics, and Lukács simply refuses to acknowledge the term's inherent slipperiness or relativity. There is no doubt, however, that Seghers has succeeded in identifying one of the weaker points of Lukács' critical method. Certainly, the notion of 'realism in general', on which Lukács pins so much of his argument, is a difficult one to sustain for very long.

Goethe and his Age

Realism intrudes too into *GA*, a collection of essays from the 1930s and 1940s dealing with some of the major figures of German classical literature – Goethe, Schiller, Lessing and Holderlin. In this attempt to prise German literature free from the clutches of the Nazis (as Lukács bitterly comments with reference to the Nazi appropriation of Holderlin, 'in the spiritual night of the fascist falsification of history, every figure becomes brown'),[7] Goethe is classified as a realist each of whose characters' lives 'arises out of real social foundations and assumptions with a genuine and true realism' (p. 56), and whose mature work 'is an organic product of his grasp of the great events of the time' (p. 16). Goethe provides us with the beginnings of great realism, his work in Lukács' opinion constituting an aesthetic bridge between the worlds of the eighteenth and nineteenth centuries and a preparation of the ground for authors such as Scott, Byron, Balzac and Stendhal. He is even referred to as the progenitor of Scott's historical novel in *Gotz von Berlichingen*. Like all great realists, Goethe's work features a discrepancy between intention and performance: he may have no great conceptual grasp of capitalist principles but his realist vision, in *Faust*, for example, enables him to express with the intuition of a poet capitalism's contradictory role in mankind's development. Goethe is accordingly enlisted in Lukács' select band of honest recorders, taking his place alongside Scott, Balzac, Tolstoy, and others.

It is at points such as this, where the concept of realism is being stretched to encompass yet another of Lukács' favourite authors, that the force of Seghers' remarks can be felt most strongly. Goethe's classicism comes from life itself and his accurate reflection of it, Lukács argues, but that does not really resolve the question why that particular reflection is so much more accurate and ideologically reliable than, say, Zola's. What is clear from both *GA* and *HN* is how seriously Lukács takes literature's role to be in the struggle to combat the hateful ideology of fascism: 'No new ideological, cultural and literary orientation is possible', he insists, 'without a new examination, a new evaluation of the world-historical currents of the past, especially the most recent past' (p. 17), and literature will be ceaselessly ransacked for what it can reveal about a world-historicality seriously out of joint. That literature counts ideologically is the gist of Lukács' arguments, and he is concerned to demonstrate to the full realism's progressive potential in a dark age. The moral seriousness of his critical project is never more obvious, or more admirable, than it is in this middle period, overshadowed by the evils of war and fascism. Realism's viability as a critical concept can come to seem a secondary consideration under these circumstances.

Defending realism: (II) post-war works

Lukács continues vigorously to press the case for realism's progressive potential in the post-war period, most notably in *The Meaning of Contemporary Realism* (1956), his most sustained engagement with the modernist movement in literature where critical realism is presented as an antidote to the modernist despair of such writers as Kafka and Beckett. One of Lukács' most controversial works, *MCR* might almost be seen as a monument to the virtues of that prototypical critical realist, Thomas Mann. Lukács' treatment of Mann's *oeuvre* in *Essays on Thomas Mann* will also be considered in this chapter, which then concludes with a look at Lukács' late study of Solzhenitsyn.

The Meaning of Contemporary Realism

Lukács insists in his preface to the German edition of *MCR* (1957) that the study contains no ideas he has not already expressed elsewhere, and while this is broadly true, we might note a different tone here from the earlier studies on realism. Both socialist realism and the cult of Stalinism are attacked more openly than before as Lukács takes advantage of the freer cultural climate in the Eastern bloc following Stalin's death in 1953, and there is a note of urgency in the way Lukács presents the book as a counter to revisionism, in his view the greatest danger currently facing Marxism. This suggests a fear on his part that the reaction against Stalin's legacy will leave the door open for a return of capitalist ideology in the field of aesthetics and elsewhere. It is against this background that Lukács' critique of modernism, that most pernicious form of capitalist aesthetic in its encouragement of personal despair and resignation in the face of socio-economic forces, needs to be viewed. Modernism has to be challenged because it is beginning to exert an appeal in the Eastern bloc, and it will be called into question by confronting it with a parallel, and allegedly healthier and morally superior tradition of writing in its own culture, critical realism.

MCR's three substantial essays investigate the ideology of modernism, the competing claims of the narrative methods of Franz Kafka and Thomas Mann, and the nature of the relationship between critical and socialist realism. Modernism is presented as in effect a surrender to the mystique of capitalism where all the system's repressive features are internalised as 'natural', critical realism as a healthy awareness of those forces within capitalist ideology that go to shape our lives. When it comes to the crunch, it is to be a choice between the world-views and the narrative methods of Franz Kafka and Thomas Mann. The terms of engagement are very similar to those of *SER* and *HN*, where the great realist novel was pitted against the novel of disillusionment, and the classical historical novel against its post-1848 biographically oriented shadow: Balzac *or* Flaubert, Scott *or* Meyer, Kafka *or* Mann, as Lukács will pose the opposition to us. Lukács makes it clear in his introduction that he regards *MCR* as a continuation of his earlier work on realism, and takes it as his task to restate the case for realism in the modern world in the face of two prejudices widely held in the bourgeois and socialist camps respectively: (1) that avant-garde modernism is the essentially modern literature; (2) that socialist realism renders critical realism obsolete. In each case Lukács scents determinism at work, with literature being held to reflect reality in an uncritical and undialectical manner: 'The formative principle of an age manifests itself in devious ways,' he warns,[1] and this is to be yet another exercise in identifying the effects of the contradictory and criss-cross currents of ideology on individual authors.

Lukács' line on modernism is an uncompromising one: 'We see that modernism leads not only to the destruction of traditional literary forms; it leads to the destruction of literature as such . . . modernism means not the enrichment, but the negation of art' (pp. 45, 46). The ideology of modernism that he seeks to challenge is that man is an alienated, ahistorical being, a fragmented personality in a fragmented world, who suffers from an acutely debilitating sense of *angst* at the meaninglessness of both his own existence and human existence in general. The modernist novel is the novel of disillusionment writ large, where mankind has long since given up the unequal struggle against the mysterious and implacable forces that control its destiny. It is the world inhabited by Kafka's K and Beckett's Molloy, one of at best an *angst*-filled existence, at worst of the utmost degradation. It is also part of the ideology of modernism not to conceive of itself as ideological and in effect to deny the sociology of literature. Lukács points out disapprovingly how obsessed bourgeois-modernist critics are with formal criteria in their discussions of the differences between modern and traditional (i.e. realist) writing, with questions of style and technique at the expense of the social dynamics, the dialectics, of literary change. For Lukács this is an approach to be avoided by the Marxist: 'We are presented with a false polarisation', he argues, 'which, by exaggerating the importance of stylistic differences, conceals the opposing principles actually underlying and determining contrasting styles' (p. 17). In other words, modernism seeks to efface its socio-political context, to reduce itself to an issue of style rather than ideology. In Lukács' terms of reference it is refusing to put reasonable questions to society and he can only oppose what to him is a surrender to the imperatives of capitalism.

Lukács is highly critical of the ontological conception of man in modernist literature and philosophy, which he compares unfavourably with that in the older realist tradition. Modernist man is alienated, solitary and asocial, incapable of establishing human relationships; realist man, on the other hand, is the traditional Aristotelian *zoon politikon*, a social animal whose ontological being cannot be distinguished from his social and historical environment – Achilles and Werther, Oedipus and Tom Jones, Antigone and Anna Karenina, to quote the examples Lukács draws from literary history. Social being determines social consciousness in the case of such realist characters, whose individuality cannot be separated from their context of creation. When any of these individuals *are* pictured as solitary it is owing to some identifiable reason in their character or social circumstances and not a condition of their being as such, a specific individual fate not a universal human condition, and the world goes on in its normal social way despite their personal experience. In sharp contrast to this state of affairs is the world of the modernist individual where solitariness is precisely the universal human condition; 'strictly confined within the limits of his own experience' (p. 21) the modernist hero is an ahistorical being who comes to realise, in the words of Thomas Wolfe quoted by Lukács, that solitariness is 'the inescapable, central fact of human existence' (p. 20). The philosophical analogue is to be found in the work of Heidegger, where man is described as having been 'thrown-into-being' in a totally arbitrary fashion that negates the possibility of meaning in human existence: 'we call it the "*thrownness*" of this entity into its "there" . . . which, as such, stares it in the face with the inexorability of an enigma.'[2] Under such circumstances there can be no change, nor hope of change in the future; only the endurance of the unpalatable fact of a meaningless existence. Such a fate to Lukács denies the very real presence of potentiality in human affairs substituting an immutable human condition in its stead. The beneficiary of this essentially static world-view, which hardly encourages the asking of awkward questions about social being or historical process, will of course be capitalism, which has everything to gain from keeping individuals confined within the limits of their own experience. We are not confronted by a scientific or a literary-critical problem in modernism, Lukács insists, but an ideological one. Whose interests, we might well query, are served by the doctrine of the essential solitariness of individual existence?

Modernism fails to give us truly typical or world-historical individuals, therefore, and its tendency (observed in the work of Musil among others) to reduce its world-view to the psychopathology of individuals means that it ends up depriving literature of all sense of perspective, of how individuals fit into the general scheme of things. When Musil has his character Ulrich, 'the man without qualities' of the novel of that name, reflect after attending the trial of the brutal murderer Moosbrugger that, 'if mankind could dream collectively, it would dream Moosbrugger,' we have just that loss of perspective that Lukács deplores.[3] In its studied lack of perspective modernism becomes the inheritor of naturalism, both styles sharing a static approach to reality. One might say that for Lukács modernism is the continuation of naturalism by other means, where the essentially naturalistic character of modernist literature is taken to be expressive of an underlying ideological continuity. Selectivity of detail, the backbone of the great realist style, is signally missing in both modernism and naturalism, and the result is that we lose any clear sense of historical change, process or necessity – precisely what made the great realist and classical historical novel of such particular value in helping us understand how society had arrived at its present state.

Rather than process we find ourselves confronted by disintegration, a profusion of worlds with little connection to each other. The reader is unable to build up any general picture of social being from these psychopathologically presented worlds, to orient herself in terms of the rest of humanity and the fluctuating current of history and ideology, which again must be seen to be in the interests of a world-dominating capitalism concerned to keep awkward questions about its method of operation to a minimum. Psychopathology functions much in the manner of biography in the later historical novel. The preference for allegory in modernist literature, Kafka providing an excellent example, is to be seen as part of an ideologically motivated desire to annihilate history, allegory presenting us with a timeless and abstract world where the concrete problems of real-life politics and ideology are not allowed to enter, where, in Kafka's bleak words, 'We are nihilistic figments, all of us; suicidal notions forming in God's mind' (quoted, p. 43). At such points the dialectics of history are being denied, and Lukács wants to leave us in no doubt as to the ideological implications of that denial: 'the destruction of literature as such' (in *SA*'s terms of reference we do not have the category of specialty), but also the destruction of opposition. The ideology of modernism is to be considered an ideology of defeat.

Modernism may have succeeded in abolishing the synthesis of universal and particular that is the essence of realism, but modernism, as Lukács makes clear in 'Franz Kafka or Thomas Mann', is not the whole story of modern literature. There is in Western culture an alternative, and vital, tradition of critical realism, whose greatest living exponent is Thomas Mann, that has at least as much claim as modernism to be considered the essentially modern literature, a claim Lukács will put to the test by comparing the respective merits of Mann and Kafka. Just as nineteenth-century literary history was reducible to a choice between the narrative practice of Balzac and Flaubert, so the twentieth century is to a choice between that of Mann and Kafka: 'the bourgeois writer today', Lukács argues, 'is in a better position to solve his own dilemma than he was in the past. It is the dilemma of the choice between an aesthetically appealing, but decadent modernism, and a fruitful critical realism. It is the choice between Franz Kafka and Thomas Mann' (p. 92).

Kafka is an author for whom Lukács has considerable respect, and whose work in many ways adheres to the realist tradition. He is, for instance, one of the few modernist writers to take a selective rather than naturalistic approach to detail, and given the stress that Lukács places on selectivity this has to be regarded as a point very much in his favour. But the principle that determines this selection, Kafka's belief in nothingness as a transcendental force, ultimately removes him from the realist camp. Kafka's artistic method may differ in detail from that of other modernist authors (the contradictory and criss-cross currents of ideology in operation), but, crucially, 'the principle of presentation is the same: the world is an allegory of transcendent Nothingness' (p. 53). Selection of detail in Kafka's case merely reveals us to be 'nihilistic figments, all of us'. In terms of the ideology of modernism what Kafka is doing is substituting his own *angst*-ridden vision of existence for objective reality, making the universal contain the special rather than the other way around, and we are on our way to the fully developed nihilistic modernism of Beckett – an author for whom Lukács is not willing to make many excuses.

Kafka's skill at communicating a sense of *angst* is freely acknowledged by Lukács, who is also prepared to admit that the experience of *angst* is an aspect of our world. But he makes a key distinction at this point which is worth dwelling on for a moment: 'The question is not: is *x* present in reality? But rather: does *x* represent the whole of reality? Again, the question is not; should *x* be excluded from literature? But rather: should we be content to leave it at *x*?' (p. 76). In other words, *angst* exists but it is not the whole story, not the only possible experience for us in the world. We should feel under no obligation as individuals to accept that as the only realistic attitude to adopt towards existence, nor the limits of our possible experience. If we leave it at *angst*, as Kafka patently does, then we merely help to perpetuate an ideological illusion whose roots can be traced back to the débâcle of 1848 and the effective division of Europe into two nations. When 'a writer takes *angst* to be the basic experience of modern man', Lukács claims, 'his attitude towards the life of his time betrays an uncritical naivety' (p. 76). Kafka and a whole host of *angst*-inspired modernist authors stand condemned of failing to paint the whole picture, of a lack of breadth of vision or willingness to go beyond their surface impressions of reality (the latter being what 'naivety' amounts to in Lukács).

Lukács treats Kafka as a classic example of a writer at the mercy of *angst*; in effect, as a writer unable to place *angst* in any kind of a social context where it could be seen for what it so obviously is to Lukács, a response to the excesses of capitalism. There is a notable discrepancy between intention and performance here: Kafka may, on the face of it, be writing about a nameless and debilitating sense of *angst* that dogs the individual, but in reality it is the pitiless world of modern capitalism that is the true subject-matter of his fiction. This is precisely what the great realists were really writing about too, but the effect of their work was to reveal this character of capitalism through the impact of social forces on their protagonists' lives, whereas in Kafka the real subject is hidden away from the audience in elliptical allegories. In *The Castle* and *The Trial* there is no sense of historical process or development, but instead only the 'vague, timeless world' of the late Hapsburg Empire, permeated by a 'haunting and indefinable' (p. 78) feeling of *angst* which is identified with the human condition in general. The ultimate effect of such fiction, it is suggested, is to induce a state of hopelessness in us and to deflect awkward questions as to how we managed to arrive in such a highly undesirable position. At that point the naivety of Kafka's work, his tendency to regard surface impressions as the whole of reality, has insidious ideological implications in terms of its impact on public consciousness.

Against this bleak vision of existence, all the more powerful in Lukács' opinion because of its ostensibly realist manner and absence of any hint of the formal experimentation taken to mar later modernist fiction, will be ranged in the work of Thomas Mann. When it comes to artistic presentation Mann immediately provides everything that a Marxist such as Lukács could wish for in a modern bourgeois realist: 'The world of Thomas Mann', he notes approvingly,

> is free from transcendental reference: place, time and detail are rooted firmly in a particular social and historical situation. Mann envisages the perspective of socialism without abandoning the position of a bourgeois, and without attempting to portray the newly emergent socialist societies or even the forces working toward their establishment. (p. 78)

We are in a real, not an allegorical world, a world peopled by typical and world-historical individuals, of diverse and conflicting viewpoints, that is presented with the breadth of vision we have come to expect from great realist writing. What Mann gives us is critical realism, a keen sense of the social pressures and historical forces that go towards forming our characters as typical and world-historical individuals. Mann for Lukács is a master at the art of selecting the typical detail that reveals the inner workings of a society: 'Each section of a portrayed totality', he points out, 'is placed in a concrete social context; the significance of each detail, its meaning for the evolution of society, is clearly defined. It is our world that Thomas Mann describes, the world in whose shaping we play a part, and which in turn shapes us' (p. 79). Lukács finds in Mann's fiction, therefore, what he so signally fails to find in the timeless, *angst*-haunted allegories of Kafka: a grasp of the dialectics of social interaction and historical process. *The Magic Mountain* may approach the condition of modernist allegory (it is set in a sanatorium sealed off from the outside world), but at least some of its characters are aware that this situation is not the norm. Mann's critical detachment contrives to keep the sanatorium experience within a wider social context, leaving it recognisably part of a larger totality (the universal being contemplated in the special not the special in the universal as in Kafka).

Even when Mann is himself exploring the darker regions of modern existence and consciousness in the novel *Dr. Faustus*, with its dabbling in the demonic in terms of the career of the avant-garde composer Adrian Leverkuhn, he is always careful to trace the social origins of all such distortions of human behaviour. Leverkuhn may seek assistance from the devil and the underworld, but it is a move he makes in response to the social conditions of his time rather than a predetermined piece of behaviour in a timeless allegory about the eternal struggle of good and evil. This enquiry into the underworld of the human mind may be set in the present, but, crucially for Lukács, it is a present seen in the wider perspective of history and thus an enquiry that succeeds in communicating a sense of historical process.

'Between these methods, between Franz Kafka and Thomas Mann', Lukács proclaims in one of those typically stark binary oppositions of his that look so increasingly questionable from a postmodern perspective, 'the contemporary bourgeois author will have to choose' (p. 80). It is a choice between what is emotively described as the 'morbidity' of formalistic experimentation for its own sake, as well as a resigned belief in *angst* as man's natural state, and the sanity associated with the progressive tradition of realism. Acceptance or rejection of *angst* is the first decision that the bourgeois author has to face, and in Lukács' scheme of things this is not primarily a literary issue but a highly significant ideological one concerning man's social being. At stake in such a decision is man's future: 'is man the helpless victim of transcendental and inexplicable forces', Lukács asks, 'or is he a member of a human community in which he can play a part, however small, towards its modification or reform?' (pp. 80–1). It is an unashamed plea on behalf of man as *zoon politikon* and of the potentiality inherent in such a condition of being. To opt for the *angst*-ridden world-view is to deny even the outside possibility of modification or reform, and to collude, however unwittingly, with the forces of reaction that want to keep the individual confined to her own limited sphere of experience. Narrative decisions, as Lukács is to insist throughout his career as a Marxist critic, are in reality *ideological* decisions and need to be analysed on that level if their full social import is to be recognised.

Lukács' fuller treatment of Mann's *oeuvre* in *ETM* will be considered shortly, but we might first consider briefly the handling of other leading modernist authors in this particular essay. Kafka, as we have seen, is by no means thought to represent modernism's worst case, and other bourgeois authors come off far less lightly from Lukács' ideologically motivated analysis. Camus, for example, is criticised for his Kafkaesque allegorical style in *La Peste*. Once again, it is the lack of perspective and development, the substitution of an abnormal interlude in human affairs for the whole story, that draws Lukács' fire. The plague is 'not shown as an accidental disaster', but as 'the reality of human existence itself, the terror of which has no beginning and no end' (p. 59). In such a setting it is not surprising if the characters' lives lack direction, motivation or development: the condition of the plague simply is the human condition, and the individual has no alternative but to struggle along as best as she can in a world controlled by transcendental and inexplicable forces. Plagues come and go, but human life remains at the mercy of their vagaries. The fact that *La Peste* has been seen by many commentators as an allegory of the German occupation of France during the Second World War simply reinforces Lukács' point: neither war nor enemy occupation need be seen as inevitable features of the human condition which we must just suffer through with a greater or lesser degree of *angst*, but as consequences of a certain kind of historical development which mankind has the power within itself to alter for the better. The note of resignation in *La Peste* is exactly what Lukács seeks to call into question in his criticism; it is yet another instance of authorial naivety, of undue and unwarranted reliance on surface impressions whose ideological implications need to be spelled out by the Marxist critic before they come to undermine our power to challenge the system that enslaves us.

Beckett, one of Lukács' *bêtes noires*, is criticised for a nihilism that can only end in stasis and silence (one can just imagine what Lukács would have made of *Breath*, a play with no characters lasting only a few seconds); Gottfried Benn (a notable collaborator with the Nazi movement) for a cynicism which can declare that 'you are what you are and you will never be different; this is, was, and always will be your life. He who has money, lives long; he who has authority; can do no wrong; he who has might, establishes right. Such is history' (quoted, p. 64), the very epitome of that ahistoricism which serves imperialist capitalism and fascism alike; D. H. Lawrence and Henry Miller for their reduction of eroticism to phallic sexuality, thus eliminating the social significance of sex; André Gide (who advocated collaboration with the occupying German forces) for a naive and uncritical fascination with the demonic side of human affairs, whereas in Thomas Mann the demonic was just one theme among many when it appeared in *Dr. Faustus*, and a theme designed to bring out mankind's latent capacity for overcoming the power of the underworld through social reformation at that. In none of these cases, save Mann of course, is the author to be considered as putting the right question to his society. Neither is it only bourgeois modernist authors who are called to account, Brecht's middle-period *Lehrstucke* – works like *The Measures Taken* or *The Mother*, for example – are regarded as attempts to impose theoretical schemes on the audience by means of characters who never rise above the level of mere spokesmen; although Brecht is thought to redeem himself in his later career and to overcome his earlier, aesthetically questionable theories and transform himself into the greatest realistic playwright of his generation. The didacticism of his middle-period offerings, however, and indeed didactic literature in general, is little to Lukács' taste, and it is that quality that he most despises in socialist realist fiction.

On the plus side of the balance sheet can be placed Conrad, a professed anti-socialist whose work eventually, and rather surprisingly, amounts to a triumph of realism, despite the fact that his narrative method prevents him from capturing life in its totality. So pared down to basics are Conrad's novels, essentially to the personal moral conflicts of their heroes (*Lord Jim* being an excellent example), that we gain a true picture of the individual under late capitalism where the system has successfully eliminated questioning of its own morality. Elsewhere Lukács can be more critical of the Conradian narrative method, complaining in *ETM* of just how much its vision excludes ('the world presented shrinks to the relationship of the isolated individual to certain isolated natural forces' (pp. 103–4)), but at least Conrad's fiction does not decline into *angst* for its own sake, and he therefore succeeds in putting some reasonable questions to his society. Eugene O'Neill is another somewhat surprising candidate for Lukács' approval, and the argument is that despite being both an experimentalist and an expressionist (neither trait likely to endear him to Lukács), he is nevertheless so heavily under the influence of nineteenth-century Ibsenite drama that he can be considered on the side of the angels: 'O'Neill wishes to know whether a man is in the last analysis responsible for his own actions or is the plaything of psychological and social forces over which he has no control,' therefore his work can be approached as a 'protest against the dominance of modernism and a confession of faith in the future of humanity' (p. 84). The Italian novelist Elsa Moranti also draws praise from Lukács. Although there would seem to be little in her work to associate her with nineteenth-century literature, Lukács detects certain affinities to an older realism none the less. Moranti's characters are rooted in a real social context and subject to real social pressures in a way that bespeaks realism rather than modernism. Even Thomas Wolfe and Norman Mailer elicit some, qualified, praise from Lukács, who shows a refreshing willingness to delve beneath the surface of the most unpromising, and ostensibly un-Marxist, material to discover what merits it might have.

By most Marxist standards Lukács' treatment of bourgeois authors is a generous one. He does not even ask that they convert to socialism: 'Not everyone who looks for a solution to the social and ideological crisis of bourgeois society – and this is necessarily the subject-matter of contemporary bourgeois literature – will be a professed socialist,' he concedes. Adding, 'It is enough that a writer takes socialism into account, and does not reject it out of hand' (p. 60). That is why a writer like Mann must continue to be of interest to the Marxist critic. Lukács remains optimistic about human nature, even when it comes to human nature in a bourgeois society. Bourgeois authors have within themselves the power to change, and if they can do that – and Lukács insists that it is perfectly possible to change one's attitude to the world around one if one really wants to do so, the forces working against the individual are by no means insurmountable – then they will gain his seal of approval. What this change will normally involve will be the rejection of the aesthetically appealing but decadent modernism of Kafka *et al.* in favour of the 'fruitful critical realism' of such as Thomas Mann, as well as a commitment not to indulge in *angst* for its own sake. In this kind of context socialist realism is not really an issue, and Lukács takes it as his brief to foster what progressive trends there are within bourgeois culture (critical realism as opposed to modernism) rather than to judge that culture by the standards of what is an alien aesthetic. He remains one of the most pragmatic of Marxist critics, who could assert in a late interview: 'I disapprove of the fact that during the Stalinist period official Marxism should have isolated itself completely from the fruits of non-Soviet developments' (*MHL*, p. 311).

The specific differences between critical realism and socialist realism are examined at greater length in *MCR*'s final essay. In terms of perspective these differences are quite marked: socialist realism takes as its perspective the struggle for socialism described from the inside, whereas critical realism will always remain outside that perspective, even when it is dealing with a socialist theme. Whether socialist realism is always true to what that perspective demands is another question, and one that Lukács proceeds to subject to some ruthless scrutiny in this essay.

Lukács is quite harsh on socialist realism overall, particularly of its Stalinist legacy of dogmatic attitudes which inhibit real critical thought. While insisting on the ultimate superiority of socialist realism over critical realism, he is also quick to point out that this superiority does not bestow automatic success on each and every product of the socialist realism school. A socialist consciousness is no guarantee of aesthetic success, therefore, and in this respect a critical realist may tell us more about our current reality than even the most politically correct Marxist author. As usual Lukács draws our attention to the problematical nature of the relationship between political consciousness and aesthetic form. 'It is no easier to translate "true consciousness" of reality into adequate aesthetic form than it is bourgeois "false consciousness",' he insists (p. 97), and he can be scathing about what the failure to realise this led to in socialist realist fiction:

> an otherwise interesting novel would be fatally marred by a scene in which a woman on a collective farm rejected the prize of a lamb she had herself brought up because communal is dearer to her heart than private property. Or a group of young Komsomols set out to win a harvest competition; they succeed in this by giving up their lunch-hour – only the strict orders of the supervisor can make them take some food and have a proper rest. The supervisor regards their zeal as an indication of the imminence of communism. Yet we are told that this collective farm is situated in a backward part of the country. (pp. 130–1)

The realist in Lukács winces at such narrative sequences, which at best are little more than wish-fulfilment failing any test of 'typicality', at worst deliberate distortions of reality which can only hinder the development of a true socialist consciousness in a society. Revolutionary romanticism of this kind merely disguises the contradictions present in a newly emerging socialist society where unequal development will be the rule. It is no more a true depiction of reality than *angst*-ridden modernism is (both can be criticised for generalising from the untypical), and it falls far behind critical realism's proven ability to foreground the internal contradictions in the disintegrating old social order as well as the emerging new one.

Lukács will always prefer the true depiction of reality, no matter what its source, and despise mere romanticism or politically correct didacticism. For that reason he argues that it is in Marxism's best interests to form a tactical alliance with critical realism, thus openly rejecting the views of those Marxists for whom socialist realism renders critical realism obsolete. An alliance with critical realism would help to rehabilitate a socialist realism which has a legacy of Stalinism to overcome, and Lukács is outspoken in his opposition to the overt schematism of the style as well as its preference for easy solutions to ideological-narrative problems. 'If a writer feels obliged, like an agitator, to supply ready solutions to all the problems of the day', he warns, 'his work will suffer' (p. 122): this will be the case whether we are dealing with a third-rate revolutionary romanticist rhapsodising about collective farms or a great writer like Brecht in the didactic mode of his *Lehrstucke*. Socialist realism ought to amount to more than ready-made solutions, and Lukács is willing to praise it when it does; but one comes out of a study like *MCR* wondering whether, protestations about innate superiority notwithstanding, Lukács really believes in socialist realism as an aesthetic theory at all. His heart seems elsewhere even when he is enumerating its virtues; there is a ritual quality about his defence of it that does not convince, that suggests expediency rather than the commitment of the true believer. He sounds infinitely more persuasive when he is detailing its shortcomings. Critical realism at its best – Thomas Mann – seems to engage his interest far more, and we can now turn to *ETM* for a fuller treatment of the figure who is the real hero of *MCR*.

Essays on Thomas Mann

Mann is established over the course of *ETM* as the most representative bourgeois writer of the first half of the twentieth century, but bourgeois though he is, Mann is a bourgeois who observes his world with an unprejudiced eye and thus attains a level of realism comparable to such masters of the past as Balzac and Stendhal: 'Posterity will be able to capture from his work with equal freshness how the typical figures of present-day bourgeois society lived, with what issues they wrestled, as they will the more distant past from the work of the great critical realists.'[4] Mann gives us society in all its contradiction, therefore; society as a site for ideological debate, social change and the workings of historical process and necessity. It is as broad a picture as we can expect to receive from within the limitations of bourgeois ideology, and it is in marked contrast to that trend in bourgeois literature, from 1848 onwards, which becomes obsessed with the meaninglessness of individual existence. In Mann's fiction there is still something at stake; it is never a case of 'you are what you are and you will never be different'; his is a world of flux from which we can learn something of human potentiality. Thus in *Dr. Faustus*, 'The ideas, the problems, the form of Adrian Leverkuhn's work are a *Summa*, an encyclopaedia of what the spirit of this age is capable of bringing forth, both for good and for bad' (p. 63). Mann's unprejudiced eye picks up the dialectics of bourgeois existence and escapes that impoverishment of post-1848 realism which culminates in the bleak landscapes of modernism and the dead end of a writer like Beckett. In Mann there is always a sense of a choice to be made between competing value systems such as capitalism and socialism.

It is the virtue of critical realism to keep debate open: Mann's fiction consistently achieves this. In *Buddenbrooks* the characters of Christian and Thomas Buddenbrooks present us with a choice between emotional anarchy and composure which faces German intellectuals at the time of writing in the early twentieth century. It is part of the paradox of early Mann, Lukács argues, that although on the surface he seems to be arguing for acceptance of 'Prussianisation' in German life, the book eventually amounts to a severe critique of the whole ethic of composure: a case of the unprejudiced eye overcoming intention in the act of performance in the very best tradition of realism. In *The Magic Mountain* we have an institution sealed off from the outside world in much the manner of modernist allegory, but Mann's critical realism turns the setting into an ideological struggle between life and death, health and sickness, and reactionary politics and democracy, to ensure that we can see the sanatorium and its inmates in a much wider social context. They are a *part* of that wider context, not a *substitute* for it as would be the case in most modernist allegories. If modernist subjectivity puts in an appearance in Mann's novels, as it does in both *The Magic Mountain* and *Confessions of Felix Krull, Confidence Man*, it is never allowed to stand for all human consciousness, but is allocated its place in the author's overall picture of present-day society, contradictory and criss-cross ideological currents and all. We can always appreciate precisely what is at stake in Mann, who is himself perpetually struggling against the forces of German history, Germany being a nation that, as Lukács points out, never really experienced bourgeois humanism as the basis of its culture, with the consequence that the 'rapid and conscious drive to decadence and reaction occurs in a purer and more complete form in Germany than in any other country' (p. 95). Germany is in fact, as a later Lukács study tells us, the home of 'the destruction of reason'. To keep debate alive within those unpromising circumstances is no mean achievement: 'No other writer', Lukács claims of Mann, 'has suffered so much from either the Germanic or the bourgeois. No-one has wrestled so unremittingly with the problems that have sprung from these closely-connected spheres' (p. 96).

It is through this struggle with a bourgeois heritage and the insistent forces that led to German fascism and the cult of unreason, that Mann is transformed into the most representative writer of his time. For all the tragedy in which his work deals, and *Dr. Faustus* is held to incarnate simultaneously the tragedy of Germany and of modern bourgeois culture as a whole, Mann still manages to leave us with some feeling of hope, the world-view of his novels ultimately being no more pessimistic, Lukács suggests, than the major tragedies of Shakespeare. Mann becomes a model of how the bourgeois author can resist the aesthetically appealing decadence of modernism with its attendant air of defeat and despair, his work a testimony to the fact that modernism is not the essentially modern literature after all.

The progressive potential of Mann's critical realism from the standpoint of dialectical materialism is self-evident after *MCR* and *ETM*. What is more contentious is whether critical realism succeeds in demolishing altogether modernism's claims on our attention. Lukács' tendency to polarise debate – Kafka *or* Mann, modernism *or* critical realism – is to be deplored for its restrictiveness, its clear suggestion that there is one, and only one, true method for the bourgeois author to follow (thus in one of his last interviews Lukács is still to be found claiming that 'We must be

clear that in every issue there is only one truth and that we Marxists are struggling for its emergence' (*MHL*, p. 326)). In its way it
is no less restrictive than the injunction laid on socialist authors to
adopt socialist realism: in neither case is the individual author left
a great deal of room for manoeuvre, for striking out on new paths
or devising new and radical methods of recording the world
around her. One must be a realist (in Lukács' admittedly quite
generous interpretation of the term) or one must incur the displeasure of the materialist critic. Lukács' essentialism remains a
stumbling block: realism is held to be the only ideologically acceptable mode of fiction writing, therefore whatever is not realism
must by definition be ideologically unacceptable. Lukács hardly
countenances the possibility that anti-realism might be ideologically subversive; rather he maintains very strict notions of how
capitalism should be challenged in fiction. The claims of the anti-
realist Marxist aestheticians (Brecht, Benjamin, Adorno, *et al.*)
that a new politics requires a new art with new forms (epic theatre,
serial music, etc.) simply falls on deaf ears in Lukács' case, and he
retains a distinctly nineteenth-century feeling to his approach to
literature in which realism is held to be morally improving and a
mark of authorial sincerity. That realism might be just one more
aesthetic construction, to be adopted or discarded as the artist sees
fit and with no intrinsic moral quality, is something that Lukács
hardly countenances either.

One might raise questions too about the rather mechanical conception of the reading process that Lukács seems to be espousing.
His main worry about modernism is that the audience will be taken
in by it, that it will become passive and resigned to its lot after
prolonged exposure to the *angst*, timeless allegories, elision of
historical process from the narrative sequence, and atypical, patho-
logically disordered characters that go to make up the standard
modernist text. But the link between text and behaviour is never
that easy to determine, and it could be argued that Lukács assumes
a very gullible and impressionable audience. One would not want
to deny that texts do affect people's behaviour or world-view –
there would be little point in writing any kind of literature otherwise – just that it is as unproblematical as Lukács would often
seem to be implying. For a critic who can be so subtle about the
relationship between a writer's ideological position and his fiction,
Lukács can be strangely blinkered on the topic of aesthetic recep-

tion. To borrow from his own terminology, the reception of literature has its contradictory and criss-cross currents no less than
ideology does. One could argue too that Lukács perhaps overestimates literature's impact on the public consciousness (his
nineteenth-century temperament showing through again perhaps);
serious literature in the twentieth century is a minority pastime
and the extent to which the works of Kafka, Joyce, Beckett *et al.*
have served to keep capitalism entrenched in the West is debata-
ble. One needs to retain a sense of perspective as to literature's
actual place in modern society and of what is at stake – how much
is at stake – in the choice of a literary style.

Where Lukács does have a point is in his refusal to accept the
modernist vision as the defining one of its time. Realism never really
went away, nor was it under any obligation to do so; nor did the
desire for linear narrative or readily comprehensible prose wither
away entirely during the reign of the modernist aesthetic. The idea
that art has to be difficult or experimental to have any claim to
seriousness or authenticity has long since been subjected to challenge by the postmodernist movement, for whom the past is still a
significant source of inspiration (if in ways that Lukács would not
always regard with approval, such as the recent fad for pastiche of
older literary styles).[5] The cult of abstraction has, for the time
being, run its course and is no longer viewed as a good in itself, a
morally superior form of artistic production in comparison to a
facile and unchallenging realism that sets its audience no particular
problems of decipherment. As for *angst*, that has ceased to be the
precondition of narrative practice, neither author nor audience
being content always to leave it at *x*, and if one were to be asked to
nominate a dominant attitude in serious literature of the late twentieth century it would most likely be irony. (It is not clear that
Lukács would have thought much of that development either, given
the hefty dose of cynicism that irony is accompanied with in so
much postmodernist fiction.) Lukács and the postmodernists though
share a belief that modernism is, ultimately, a dead end, both emotionally and stylistically (follow the path of Beckett and post-*Breath*
there is, literally, no place to go, silence and stasis reign); although it
should also be pointed out that the more iconoclastic of the postmodernists – Lyotard, for example – hold the same to be true of
Marxism (for the ex-Marxist Lyotard, an outmoded and discredited
'grand narrative' deserving no further public support).

The reasons for problematising modernism may differ, but there are points of contact to note between Lukács and the post-modernist movement which are worth exploring and to which we shall return in the closing chapter. At the very least one can say that the advent of postmodernism has meant that Lukács' critique of modernism no longer looks as idiosyncratic and reactionary as it once undoubtedly did: realism and the past still have some aesthetic mileage left in them.

Solzhenitsyn

Stalinism and socialist realism loom large on the agenda of Lukács' late study on Solzhenitsyn. Lukács regards it as the central problem of modern socialist realism to come to terms with the Stalinist era, that era which shook so many people's faith in socialism and whose repercussions were still to be felt in Eastern bloc life at the book's time of writing in the 1960s. He considers Solzhenitsyn to be one of the few writers successfully to make the attempt. It is Solzhenitsyn's great virtue that in works like *One Day in the Life of Ivan Denisovich*, *The First Circle* and *Cancer Ward*, 'he gives clear and convincing compendia of the inhibiting after-effects of the Stalinist period',[6] and it will be his talent for this, as well as the implications it holds for the future of socialist realism, that comes under closest scrutiny in the study. Solzhenitsyn provides no solutions to the various problems that Stalinism poses for socialism, but, as usual, that is not a requirement Lukács lays on the author of fiction: 'the duty of the genuine writer', he observes, with the negative experience of Stalinist-era socialist realism etched deeply in his memory, 'is to concentrate on intensive questions and not on direct answers' (p. 87). Such intensive questions abound in Solzhenitsyn's fiction.

Considerable claims are made for Solzhenitsyn. Not only does he represent a new development in the history of socialist realism, his works are also argued to be 'undoubtedly the first and most important precursors of a new creative epoch' (p. 87). It is as if Lukács finally has found someone on his own side of the fence to measure up to Thomas Mann, although it is significant, given his often ambivalent response to socialist realism, that it requires a departure from what we might call 'classical' socialist realism

before such an event can occur. One of the clear differences between the two forms of socialist realism is Solzhenitsyn's refusal to
provide ready-made solutions, and Lukács is as critical as ever of
what he takes to be the detrimental effect of propaganda on narrative: 'in the Stalinist period, the political character of literature
became manifest in its obligation to provide definite and concrete
guidelines for the solution of certain current political problems' (p.
77). The relationship between politics and narrative form in Solzhenitsyn is much more oblique than this, to the benefit of his work
both as fiction and as a record of its age. There is to be no decline
into the crudely manipulative 'illustrating literature' of the Stalinist era, a literature that presented the world as the political authorities wanted it to be (full of self-sacrificing collective farm
members and atypically eager young Komsomols) and not as it was
in reality.

Another critical difference between Solzhenitsyn and classical
socialist realism lies in his use of the novella form. Novellas, as
Lukács points out, deal with single situations, and in terms of plot
and characterisation tend to remain fixed at that level, as we can
observe in *Ivan Denisovich*. In the normal run of things Lukács is
no particular fan of the novella, which by realist standards offers a
restricted range of experience and which in the hands of many
bourgeois authors, Hemingway and Conrad being cases in point,
represents something of an admission of ideological defeat, 'a re-
arguard action in their struggles for the deliverance of man' (p.
10). Solzhenitsyn's type of novella, however, escapes this trap. It
does not constitute, as Conrad and Hemingway's do, a retreat from
the novel form and its unique breadth of vision, but rather an
'initial exploration of a reality in the search for the great forms
appropriate to it' (p. 15). It is as if Solzhenitsyn has come to realise
that he is in uncharted territory and can no longer rely on the
accredited forms of the past – forms which had been subject to so
much abuse in the era of classical socialist realism. The new epoch
for socialist realism begins with that realisation, and Lukács is
happy to sanction such a break with the past, insisting that the
times demand a change in authorial approach, that the socialist
realism of today should be developing a style different in character
to the one originally conceived as a response to the reality of the
1920s. It can sometimes seem as if Lukács cannot see past the great
realist novel style as the all-purpose answer to the recording of

reality in fiction, but here in late career, confronted by the Solzhenitsyn novella, he gives every impression of making a conscious effort to be more flexible in his literary aesthetic, of allowing historical process into the development of prose fiction. The havoc wreaked by Stalinism and its legacy in socialist life is so extreme that it requires a rethinking of approach in all areas, including aesthetics.

The study is in two parts; the first, written in 1964, deals with *Ivan Denisovich*, and the second, from 1969, looks at *The First Circle* and *Cancer Ward*. Whereas in the first essay Solzhenitsyn is regarded as a writer of considerable promise, by the second Lukács is declaring that Solzhenitsyn has brought about a rebirth of socialist realism. Although the setting of *Ivan Denisovich*, the enclosed world of a Soviet labour camp under Stalin, suggests the world of modernist allegory (recalling the way enclosed communities function in works like Camus' *La Peste*), Lukács resists classifying it that way. The work is not symbolically conceived, he argues, although he will admit that it is capable of exerting a strong symbolic effect on the reader. Despite the fact that it makes no attempt to evoke the wider reality of the world of Stalinist Russia outside the camp, nevertheless camp life is an implicit commentary on that world. One might wonder how this differs from the condition of allegory, and it has to be said that Lukács is not entirely convincing here. He even concedes that *Ivan Denisovich* lacks perspective, one of the great sins of modernist writing if we recall *MCR*, although Lukács does argue that 'the austere abstinence from any perspective itself contains a concealed perspective' (p. 22) – but then one could also say the same of almost any modernist (or naturalist) work. Behind the apparently perspectiveless world of Kafka's fiction lies the perspective that 'we are nihilistic figments, all of us'; behind the scientifically clinical eye of Zola is the perspective that the socio-economic forces of modern capitalist life are crushing the individual spirit. The anti-allegory reading of *Ivan Denisovich* seems to depend on the quality of the narrative's realistic detail, with its ability to evoke the stark alternative consistently facing the camp's inmates between survival and going under. There is, in other words, a social context of some sort and a concrete situation for the characters to respond to: freefloating *angst* has no place in such a setting. Neither is this a world ruled by a sense of resignation to one's fate, the exigencies of survival are too keen for that and prevent *Ivan Denisovich*'s characters from declining into mere 'nihilistic figments'. Survival has an important social dimension in the narrative, it is not just a case of the isolated individual versus brute natural forces as it is in *Typhoon* or *The Old Man and the Sea*. If this is a depressing world, it is so for concrete and highly visible reasons rather than through some nameless dread generated by mysterious and inexplicable forces outside human control, and consequently is not to be confused with the world of modernist allegory where the universal is made to subsume the special. Lukács complains that 'the nothingness of a Beckett . . . is a mere game with fictitious abysses that no longer correspond to anything of importance in historical reality' (p. 28), but Solzhenitsyn's work, for all its surface resemblances to modernist allegory, remains anchored in a specific historical reality (implicitly rather than explicitly signalled to the reader) whose abysses are all too real.

In steering away from modernist allegory Lukács comes uncomfortably close to a naturalist interpretation of the novella. The reference to abstinence from perspective in particular suggests this, conjuring up the narrative world of Zola. When Lukács speaks of the work as a 'limited slice of life' (p. 23) and of the 'non-interpretative descriptive methods' (p. 26) by which it is achieved, he seems to move further towards *Ivan Denisovich* as naturalist narrative. Clearly this would not be an acceptable conclusion to reach since naturalism is felt to serve the interests of capitalism not socialism, and Lukács wants to insist that Solzhenitsyn's work has nothing in common with the naturalist aesthetic; nevertheless he has to work quite hard to rescue *Ivan Denisovich* from the charge and the argument has its gaps. The limited slice of life is said to be presented with an economy that distinguishes it from the profusion of detail of an author like Zola: each detail counts as it is always made to do in Mann or any other realist of note, and the effect is to make us appreciate its significance in the overall narrative scheme of things. There is to be nothing gratuitous in the Solzhenitsyn novella: 'Every detail presents an alternative between survival and succumbing' (p. 20) in camp life. The descriptive methods may be non-interpretative but they also succeed, Lukács argues, in revealing what is typical in the details presented (exactly why the particular set of details chosen by a naturalist author fails to do the same is no clearer here than it was in *MCR* however).

The overall effect is to establish camp life, in all its 'mean, threadbare reality', as a totality, 'a humanly significant symbolic totality which illuminates an important aspect of human life' (p. 20), and as we know, totality is the ultimate goal of artistic endeavour to Lukács, the arrival at the category of specialty.

The typicality of the struggle to survive against powerful forces which have a human rather than a metaphysical basis is the typicality of a Stalinist era reality, and Solzhenitsyn brings to life this mean, threadbare reality with great skill and economy. Rather like Scott, Solzhenitsyn has a particular talent for rendering historical crisis through the experience of typical individuals. The characters of camp life, ordinary and unremarkable individuals in the main, are caught up and implicated in a historical process which permeates every area of Soviet life, and Solzhenitsyn shares with Scott and the classical historical novel a skill for creating situations which force the characters to reveal the nature of their relations to the rest of society. Such characters may fail to provide solutions to the socio-historical crisis within which they find themselves, but their actions, their perpetual struggle for survival, keep the questions put to them by their social existence in the foreground of the reader's consciousness. On those combined grounds of economy, lack of gratuitous detail and sense of socio-historical process and typicality (however obliquely these may be registered) Solzhenitsyn can be absolved of all charges of naturalism. In Solzhenitsyn's novella, unlike the novellas or the naturalist novels of the bourgeoisie, we are kept aware of the Marxist maxim that 'man makes his own history': and in many ways that is the great tragedy of the Stalinist period that his work unfolds. It could, it should, have been all so very different, and literature's surrender to the demands of the Stalinist propaganda machine merely exacerbated the process whereby the wrong history was made. Dishonest recording has serious ideological implications.

Lukács considers that *The First Circle* and *Cancer Ward* amply fulfil the promise of *Ivan Denisovich*, and reveal Solzhenitsyn to be the true heir not just of socialist realism but of the great Russian literary tradition of Tolstoy and Dostoevsky. In *The First Circle* we are concerned again with an enclosed group of characters – privileged specialists working in secrecy preparing inventions for the Stalinist regime – but in this case we are given an explicit sense of the wider reality within which this group functions, the Stalinist hierarchy where the 'behavioural requirements made of every character in consequence of his position on the bureaucratic ladder' and the 'consequence of individual personal reactions to these requirements' (p. 51) are painstakingly recorded. The novel becomes an exploration of the effect of the Stalinist principle of bureaucratisation on typical lives and how this reduces most such lives to a series of tactical responses to the wishes of the hierarchy. Solzhenitsyn makes it clear how typicality is distorted by the bureaucracy, which is given back only the message that it wants to hear. The substitution of bureaucratic principles for socialist principles and the way that this exchange obscures the dynamics of historical process is a fit subject for socialist realism. Lukács himself had drawn attention to the dangers such a cultural phenomenon posed for socialist development in the 1940 essay 'Tribune or Bureaucrat?' (with its ambivalent treatment of Stalin's role in the process), but it has taken until Solzhenitsyn for those dangers to find their true fictional form. *The First Circle* constitutes a devastating critique of Stalinism's construction of its own self-enclosed reality and thus answers Lukács' call for a new kind of socialist realism willing to ask intensive questions of the Stalinist era. *Cancer Ward*, set in the troubled period following Stalin's death, asks just as intensive and penetrating questions about Soviet society's attempts to come to terms with Stalin's legacy, and is just as acute in revealing social contradictions, and as short on solutions to them, as the other fictions proved to be.

Lukács is willing to allow considerable latitude to the new kind of socialist realism including dispensing with that great realist precondition, the unified plot. It is enough that the setting of the narrative, even if it is rendered in apparently unrelated individual scenes, generates reactions in the characters whose totality reveals. the social forces behind that setting. Thus the individual scenes of a Solzhenitsyn narrative collectively add up to a totality of reactions to the phenomenon of Stalinism. As long as the characters are aware of some disparity between their own world-view and that of the system that confronts them, as Solzhenitsyn's typical characters are in terms of the Stalinist bureaucracy, then there need be no unity of plot, a unity of reactions will suffice to underpin the author's critique. Instead of the static world-view that an absence of unified plot led to in naturalism, there will be a narrative with the dynamics that realism demands: 'although (or precisely because) the reactions triggered reveal the greatest dissimilarities, even antitheses, dramatically moving, uniformly narrative connections can originate in individual scenes which appear to be unrelated', Lukács points out, adding that, 'these connections can then be combined by narrative means into a totality of human reactions to an important problem complex' (p. 43), such as Stalinism presents. Given honest recording of the reactions in the individual scenes then we need not make a fetish of unified plot, and this represents a significant gesture on Lukács' part in the direction of aesthetic flexibility. Realism can incorporate more modern narrative methods as long as these help to reveal historical process, change and necessity at work in a society.

The Solzhenitsyn study makes it clear that Lukács conceives of realism as a living and constantly developing tradition. Critical realism and socialist realism both can, and should, change in response to the world around them, the only requirement being laid on their practitioners that they record the reality of that world as honestly as they can in terms of the experience of typical not atypical characters. The value of realism can be seen to reside in that honest picture, especially when constructed against the grain of political prejudice or the insensitivities of bureaucratic diktat, with its unrivalled capacity to bring the contradictory and criss-cross currents of ideology to the reader's attention. It will never be a case of what solutions realist authors, of whatever persuasion, offer to socio–political problems, that is not literature's role as Lukács repeatedly emphasises, but of the questions they manage to raise about their society and its ideological basis. By posing appropriately awkward and intensive questions, realism delivers a way into the inner workings of a society and its ideology, hence its importance for the Marxist cultural analyst. Throughout the course of his various studies on realism, Lukács never loses that belief in realism's unique ability to keep historical process, change and necessity firmly in the foreground of the reader's consciousness.

CHAPTER

SIX

Lukács and Brecht

The idea that realism should be the basis of a Marxist aesthetic was not universally accepted on the left, even though it became official Soviet policy in the 1930s. By then a counter-tradition was well established in the West which took exception to the realist line, arguing that art should be experimental and formally challenging, not rooted in past styles and conventions. As Brecht, one of the leading lights of this movement, put it: 'For time flows on . . . . Methods become exhausted; stimuli no longer work.'[1] Modernist, or anti-realist, Marxist aesthetics was based on the premiss that a new and radical politics demanded a new and radical art. It was the duty of the artist to challenge the existing order in the art world and to reject methods and styles associated with the bourgeois past (as realism clearly was). Such ideas had been rampant in post-revolutionary Russia, which for a while in the 1920s had been a hothouse of artistic experimentation, but the dead hand of Stalinism ultimately descended and socialist realism became the norm with dissenting voices being silenced. In the West, however, such figures as Brecht, Benjamin and the various members of the Frankfurt School (Adorno, Marcuse, Horkheimer) continued to argue the case for a modernist Marxist aesthetic. Lukács was a bitter opponent of this tendency and regarded it as an unhealthy development within Marxism. Brecht and Lukács come to symbolise the divide in Marxist aesthetics during the 1930s and their opposing views will be considered here.

Brecht is one of the great innovators of twentieth-century theatre and his 'epic theatre' is deliberately non-realistic in style, doing all it can to distance itself from a realism that Brecht regards as ideologically suspect and aesthetically exhausted. The basis of epic theatre is the 'alienation effect' whereby the audience is prevented from being drawn into any illusion of reality on stage by a variety of disruptive techniques – songs, stylised acting, unrealistic costume and scenery, use of other media such as cinematic projection, visible stage machinery, etc. Brechtian theatre is out to make political points, not to offer escapist entertainment, and it views realism as both bourgeois and escapist. Formal experimentation is for Brecht an anti-bourgeois gesture of conspicuously political intent. As his friend and collaborator the critic Walter Benjamin put it, 'We must rethink the notions of literary forms or genres if we are to find the forms appropriate to the literary energy of our time. Novels did not always exist in the past, nor must they necessarily always exist in the future.'[2] A similar point is made by another of the prominent Marxist modernists, Theodor Adorno, when he attacks the continued reliance of so many twentieth-century composers on nineteenth-century harmonic structures:

> All the tonal combinations employed in the past by no means stand indiscriminately at the disposal of the composer today. Even the more insensitive ear detects the shabbiness and exhaustion of the diminished seventh chord and certain chromatic modulatory tones in the salon music of the nineteenth century. . . . The most progressive level of technical procedures designs tasks before which traditional sounds reveal themselves as impotent.[3]

The 'progressive' level in this instance is the demanding music of Arnold Schoenberg, with its rejection of tonality in favour of the twelve-tone system of composition and its very different sound-world – an emotionally unsettling sound-world far more in keeping with the traumatic socio-political landscape of the twentieth century as far as Adorno is concerned. In each case the point being made is that a new social situation requires a new artistic language, a self-consciously radical one that deliberately severs itself from tradition and all its adverse political connotations. Tradition is seen to be a stumbling block to the creation of a new society with a new consciousness, and modernist Marxist artists, therefore, must oppose it in the most effective way they can – through revolutionising the form of their art. Formal experimentation is transformed into a political statement.

There is an iconoclastic quality to modernist Marxist aesthetics that is anathema to a critic like Lukács, for whom the past is the key to an understanding of historical process and who goes out of his way to insist on Marxism's respect and admiration for the classical heritage of mankind. Cutting oneself off from the past in the manner of a Brecht, a Benjamin or an Adorno is effectively to cut oneself off from historical process, at which point alarm bells start ringing for the Marxist cultural historian. There is also the problem that experimental art tends to have minority appeal, and that does not fit in easily with the realist demand for an accessible art which speaks to all mankind ('Art belongs to the people. Its roots should penetrate deeply into the very thick of the masses of the people. It should be comprehensible to the masses and loved by them,' in Lenin's emphatic words).[4] In Lukács' view what we are presented with in modernist literature is not the typical experience of mankind but the atypical, and this lacks the universal significance (and wide accessibility) that he considers to be the hallmark of great art – indeed, of entry to the category of specialty. Brecht's insistence on the popularity and working-class appeal of his own work is an attempt to combat the realists on their own ground, although not a wholly successful one since his Weimar Republic audience was predominantly bourgeois in composition and the *Lehrstucke* were hardly classifiable as popular works. Even if Brecht's claims could be substantiated, they would be unlikely to allay Lukács' fears as to the negative impact the presentation of atypical experience could have on an audience.

Lukács was a highly visible figure on the German literary left in the 1930s. After abandoning active politics in the HCP in the wake of the furore over the 'Blum Theses' in 1929, he eventually moved to Berlin after a brief sojourn in Moscow and became closely involved with *Linkskurve*, the journal of the Association of Proletarian-Revolutionary Writers. Lukács was soon one of its most influential contributors, stirring up considerable controversy with his pro-realist views. One of his early targets was the novelist Ernst Ottwalt, a collaborator of Brecht's (they scripted a film together), and the critique of Ottwalt's *Denn sie wissen* in 'Reportage or Portrayal' led Lukács into open confrontation with Brecht, whose play *The Measures Taken* is criticised for being an exercise in abstract preaching. It is not hard to identify what Lukács would object to in a piece like the latter, with its thin, even non-existent characterisation and lack of any really meaningful social context. Both Brecht and Ottwalt are guilty as Lukács sees it of adopting an 'anti-portrayal' style which reveals them to have an undialectical historical consciousness. In Lukácsian terms of reference *The Measures Taken* would be no more than the bare bones of a play. Brecht might also have felt himself to be under attack in Lukács' later essay 'Expressionism: its significance and decline' (1934), a vigorous assault on the expressionist legacy in German literature, with its claim that expressionism helped pave the way for fascism. Although not mentioned by name, Brecht could be considered implicated as one who began his playwriting career in the expressionist style (*Baal*, for example). Certainly Brecht perceived Lukács as a threat to his own position on the left; as Benjamin remarked in his diary in 1938, 'The publications of Lukács, Kurella [an associate of Lukács] *et al.* are giving Brecht a good deal of trouble.'[5] Later in the same year, Benjamin reports Brecht's assessment of Lukács and his associates in Moscow as 'enemies of production'. 'Production', Brecht continues, 'makes them uncomfortable. You never know where you are with production; production is the unforseeable. You never know what's going to come out. And they themselves don't want to produce. They want to play the *apparatchik* and exercise their control over other people. Every one of their criticisms contains a threat.'[6] This is slightly unfair on Lukács, who is being lumped together with the Zhdanovite tendency he so despised, but it does hint at a more uneasy relationship between art and politics than most realists were willing to admit.

Lukács does alter his opinion on Brecht in later life, perhaps not unmindful of the fact that after his return to East Germany in the late 1940s Brecht, in his guise as director of the Berliner Ensemble, became one of the cultural heroes of the Eastern bloc. It is significant, however, that Lukács can only praise Brecht on the basis of the supposed greater realism of his later plays (*Mother Courage*, for example) where the characters are held to be multidimensional: the dislike for the earlier *Lehrstucke* remains. Whether multidimensionality was something that Brecht was striving for in a play like *Mother Courage* is, however, very much a moot point.

Brecht's most sustained response to the 'good deal of trouble' that Lukács was setting him was a series of pieces intended for publication in the emigré German literary periodical *Das Wort*, published in Moscow. In the event these were not published in Brecht's lifetime and first appeared in English in 1974 under the title 'Against Lukács'. In the course of these short pieces Brecht mounts a savage attack on the theory of realism, which he regards as having a stultifying effect on literary endeavour. The claim is that the theory is narrow, being based on a very select group of narrative models, over-obsessed with characterisation and the need to create enduring figures, reactionary in the extreme in its refusal to countenance experiments with form, and too rigid to be any guide to literary practice in a rapidly changing socio-political situation. Brecht points out, quite correctly, that Lukács grounds the theory on the practice of a small band of novelists. We have seen how the same names keep recurring throughout the various studies on realism – Scott, Balzac, Stendhal, Tolstoy, Gorki and Mann on the plus side, Flaubert, Hugo, Zola and Kafka on the minus. The injunction this places the modern author under, Brecht argues, is to 'Be like Tolstoy – but without his weakness! Be like Balzac – only up-to-date.'[7] Such an injunction is restrictive to the artistic imagination which likes, even needs, to take risks. Artists, Brecht pleads, have to be given free rein: 'we shall allow the artist to employ his fantasy, his originality, his humour, his invention . . . we shall not bind the artist to too rigidly defined rules of narrative.'[8] The argument has some similarities to the Romantic reaction against neoclassicism, an aesthetic theory claiming to derive eternal 'laws' of narrative from a small group of classical authors (Homer and Virgil above all), which eventually ossified into a set of restrictive practices jealously guarded by a cultural police. Brecht is just as worried at the assumption of eternal aesthetic laws from the work of a few approved nineteenth-century novelists whose experience was so different from his own: 'Frankly I myself learn more easily where problems similar to my own are confronted. Not to beat about the bush, I learn with more difficulty (less) from Tolstoy and Balzac. They had to master other problems.'[9] This is not an argument against Tolstoy and Balzac, just against the idea that their narrative procedures are endlessly recyclable no matter what the social situation facing the writer. Put like this, Lukács seems to be falling into exactly the sins he most deplores – ahistoricism and formalism: 'Realism is not a mere question of form,' Brecht argues. 'Were we to copy the style of these realists, we would no longer be realists.'[10]

Brecht is also highly critical of Lukács' obsession with characterisation, more precisely with a certain kind of characterisation: the well-rounded character who turns into an 'enduring figure'. Creating a character who becomes a byword (Quixotic, Scrooge-like) is a mark of literary success in Lukács' opinion, proof positive that the author has managed to capture a sense of 'typicality' that the audience instantly recognises as true to its real-life experience. It is the category of specialty showing its true value. Brecht claims to put no great value on the quality of endurance, insisting, quite rightly, that there is no way of telling how long the endurance will last anyway. Whether a Balzac or Tolstoy character will endure indefinitely no one can say, nor does Brecht see why twentieth-century literary techniques, montage for example, should be judged by such standards: modern authors' interests simply lie elsewhere than in the creation of durable characters. The cult of the individual, of which the durable literary character is one manifestation, is a class-based phenomenon and not one that socialists should be aiding and abetting. It is false, Brecht contends, for the writer 'to simplify his problems so much that the immense, complicated, actual life-process of human beings in the age of the final struggle between the bourgeois and the proletarian class, is reduced to a "plot", setting, or background for the creation of great individuals.'[11] Once again Lukács stands accused of ahistoricism, of remaining stuck in an essentially nineteenth-century frame of reference, which has limited relevance to current socio-political realities.

Brecht is adamant that the writer must be given the chance to experiment, even to fail. Some experiments may come to nothing, others may take a while for their potential to become clear, but it is far preferable to struggle to come to terms with an ever-changing reality than merely to recycle older methods of doing so: 'We must not derive realism as such from particular existing works, but we shall use every means, old and new, tried and untried, derived from art and derived elsewhere, to render reality to men in a form they can master.'[12] This right to experiment, right to fail, can only

clash with the critical desire to control aesthetic effect and indicates again the essentially uneasy relationship between art and
politics.

Overall, Brecht suggests that realism as defined by Lukács is
simply too narrow a concept to guide writers in the turbulent
socio-political climate of 1930s Europe: 'For time flows on . . . .
Methods become exhausted; stimuli no longer work.' Audiences,
Brecht claims, particularly proletarian audiences, can spot the
worn-out and the clichéd, and want to be challenged by works of
art. Indeed challenge becomes the basis for his aesthetic: a work 'so
commonplace that it no longer made one think, they did not like at
all ("You get nothing out of it"). If one needed an aesthetic, one
could find it here.'[13] Brecht makes the entirely reasonable point
that realism was a new style in its own time and needed to overcome older styles; modernism is in exactly that position now, and
that is a necessary process if literature is to keep pace with the
rapid development of reality. For Lukács to deny this is for him to
lapse into ahistoricism, and indeed he can suggest an undialectical
perspective when it comes to the subject of realism, as when he
remarks, in an essay on Pushkin, that 'realism is not a style but the
social basis of every truly great literature' (*WC*, p. 231).

Brecht's critique of realism is a persuasive one even if it often
overstates the case. Lukács did not, for example, advocate that
novels should be simply backgrounds for the creation of great
individuals, in fact he opposed that procedure, arguing that novels
should communicate a sense of historical process through the experience of typical individuals (he did allow great individuals to be
the basis of drama, however). He was quite happy for the protagonist to be a commonplace personality – as we saw in the case of his
reading of Scott – as long as the workings of historical process
registered clearly. Neither did he advocate the simple reproduc-
tion of nineteenth-century realism in a twentieth-century context,
he admitted the need for change and was quick to praise authors
who found ways of extending realism's palette – Thomas Mann
being the obvious case in point. Nevertheless Brecht does succeed
in drawing blood on occasion. Realism is a relatively safe option
for the author, even if she is extending its palette, and it does bear
the stamp of bourgeois culture. To admit the latter point, as
Lukács himself does, is to admit tacitly that realism is not an
eternally valid or 'natural' style, and Brecht does pinpoint a very

real contradiction in Lukács' thought, where the concept of realism is not being viewed as historically as it should be. The suggestion of a formalist bias to Lukács' literary aesthetic hits home too, and essentialism remains one of Lukács' weak spots. Brecht also makes the telling point that the novel cannot be regarded as a model for all other kinds of literary activity: Lukács is guilty of illicitly collapsing literary history into the history of the novel.

What one can say overall, however, is that Lukács still shows the greater grasp of historical process, of how the past sets the agenda for the present. Brecht's attitude is far more iconoclastic, and he is too prone to dismiss the past as of no interest to us now. Perhaps this need to feel unencumbered by history and tradition was necessary for his own creative process, but it is a weak basis for a general aesthetic theory. There is also an element of romanticisation in Brecht's picture of a proletarian audience craving to be challenged by the artist. Aesthetic conservatism is no less a feature of this audience than a middle-class bourgeois one. We come down to the basic split in Marxist aesthetics between a belief in art as disorienting and provocative and art as accessible. The problem of course is that it is seen in such a mutually exclusive way: *either* modernism *or* realism, *either* Brecht *or* Lukács. Marxist aesthetics never quite overcomes that division, although the idea that radical art will have a generally liberating political effect tends to be viewed with more scepticism on the left nowadays. As a recent commentator on Herbert Marcuse, who maintained a firm belief in the political significance of radical art to the end of his life, put it, 'it is really time to recognize that formal experimentation will not *necessarily* have a more critical and emancipatory content than a representational emphasis upon content'.[14] Postmodernism has further encouraged this view, and although the underlying aesthetic involved is very different from Marxist realism (there can often be an element of cynicism which Lukács would have abhorred), it has nevertheless brought representationalism and realism back onto the cultural agenda. Lukács cannot simply be dismissed on the grounds of his conservatism, and in many ways is a more reliable guide than Brecht or any of the modernists as to how literature actually is received in the public domain.

CHAPTER SEVEN | *Lukács' political writings*

Lukács' direct involvement in politics occurred during the years 1919–29, when he was an important figure in the Hungarian Communist Party, and then more briefly in 1956, which saw him a member of the ill-fated Nagy government of the Hungarian uprising. He produced a considerable body of political essays over the course of that first political period, less in later life (after the fuss concerning the 'Blum Theses' Lukács effectively retired from active political life until joining the Nagy government as its Minister of Culture), although he returned to political matters on occasion, most notably on the vexed subject of Stalin and his bitter legacy for socialism. This chapter will consider the early political writings, including the ill-starred 'Blum Theses', and then some of the later reflections on Stalin, particularly 'Tribune or Bureaucrat?' (1940), one of the most tortuous pieces of writing in the Lukács canon in terms of its political line.

Early political writings

The first point to register about the early political writings, in Rodney Livingstone's collected edition,[1] is the cultural climate in which they were composed. This was a heady period in Marxist history, with a successful social revolution accomplished in Russia, various others revolutions sporadically breaking out around Europe, and a Soviet government to coordinate the class struggle worldwide. For at least a few years, with the old order showing signs of serious strain, almost anything seemed possible as far as Marxists were concerned. Lukács' early political writings reflect the sense of urgency and rapidly changing socio-political situation of the time in the way that they address political concerns of immediate and practical interest: how the Communist Party should be organised, what strikes it should and should not support, how it should respond to events elsewhere.[2] It is also important to note how pragmatic a political thinker Lukács can be. Situations are to be assessed on their merits and not with the eye of a romantic revolutionary impatient for immediate success or a dogmatist concerned to protect the purity of Marxist theory (thus Lukács can oppose cooperation with communism's opponents at one point but urge it at another when communism is in a weaker political position); the need for tactics is constantly stressed ('the revolutionary experiences of recent years have demonstrated clearly the *limits of revolutionary spontaneity*' he observes in 1921 ('Spontaneity of the Masses, Activity of the Party', p. 101)); Hungary's social backwardness is held to necessitate a democratic interim before the establishment of the dictatorship of the proletariat will be possible. Lukács' faith in the communist cause never wavers but he is no dogmatist as to how the class struggle is to be waged or the triumph of Marxism achieved:

> Therefore, to weigh up and understand correctly the contemporary economic and social conjuncture, the true relations of power, is never more than to meet the *prerequisites* for correct socialist action, correct tactics. It does not in itself constitute a *criterion* of correctness. The *only* valid yardstick is whether the *manner* of the action in a given case serves to realize this goal.   ('Tactics and Ethics', p. 5)

It is the authentic voice of the critic who was later to insist that political correctness was no guarantee of literary realism, and it consistently leads Lukács into conflict with his fellow party members in the period, who show an increasing inclination towards dogmatism as the 1920s progress. The rows over *HCC* and the 'Blum Theses' were to be merely the opening rounds in a life-long battle between Lukács and the dogmatists of Marxist thought.

Here, as elsewhere in his writings, Lukács lays great stress on the need to remain aware at all times of historical process. Not to do so is undialectical, and we see him mounting a prescient attack on the tendency, later to culminate in the nightmare of Stalinism, to fall into just that trap: 'Unable to comprehend Hegel's conception of history' certain post-Hegelian dialectical theorists 'have turned historical development into a wholly automatic process, not only independent of, but even qualitatively different from consciousness' ('"Intellectual Workers" and the Problem of Intellectual Leadership', p. 16). Such automatic processes do not exist for Lukács, they need to be fought for by real individuals working together within specific historical situations: this is the message of Marx and Engels, 'man makes his own history', and it is one that Marxists neglect at their peril. Stalin is soon to do so, with drastic consequences for the history of socialism. Even at this early point in his career Lukács shows himself keenly conscious of the determinist dangers lurking within dialectical theory, and he will be a consistent opponent of such vulgar interpretations of Marxism. Throughout these early political writings there is a distinct sense of someone struggling to combat adverse trends within Marxism itself which work to negate the theory's socially revolutionary potential. Determinism is the enemy within, dialectical awareness of historical process by the party *and* the proletariat the means of keeping it at bay. These are themes which will resound through Lukács' work.

Awareness of historical process is also an awareness of the complex dialectical relationship between the party and the proletariat, and Lukács is much exercised by this issue throughout these writings. It is a relationship which much troubles Marxist theorists from this point onwards, and a tendency develops to put the party first. Lukács sounds a prophetic warning against such undialectical behaviour which cuts against the workings of historical process, change and necessity: 'Where a party seriously believes that it "stands above and beyond the classes", it condemns itself from the outset to inactivity' ('Party and Class', p. 31). The view of the proletariat in these essays is very much that of *HCC*: it is a class with a world-historical mission to rescue mankind from capitalism, and it is the duty of the party to help the proletariat realise its potential for social change (otherwise the latter might lapse into a counter-productive anarchic spontaneity of action). Neither should be seen in isolation from the other but as interdependent elements in an evolving socio-historical process:

> the antagonism between the actions of the class and the actions of the party is anything but clear-cut, with one side obviously right and the other equally obviously wrong. Rather it is a dialectical antagonism, one in which both forms of action, although mutually exclusive and opposed to each other, are yet equally necessary . . . the existence of the one demands the existence of the other.   (*Ibid.*, p. 30)

The intensely dialectical character of Lukács' thought is very apparent at such points. He is no believer in easy short-cuts to dialectical success. The keenly sought unity of party and proletariat, the Hegelian sublation of all the contradictions present in that often awkward relationship, cannot be achieved by party diktat, due process must be observed.

Marxism is above all a process to Lukács rather than a series of timeless truths and he attacks the idea that the party can be in possession of such truths as undialectical, remarking in an essay on Rosa Luxembourg that she 'was never concerned to pronounce "timeless", "eternally valid" truths; on the contrary, she attempted to determine, by concrete analysis of concrete historical situations, the tactics necessary at those particular times' ('Spontaneity of the Masses', p. 97). The preference for concrete analysis of concrete historical situations over supposedly timeless truths is one that Lukács is to maintain no matter what his object of enquiry – politics, literature or philosophy – but one cannot always say the same of Marxist thought in general, particularly in the Soviet Union and the Eastern bloc. The party does begin to dominate and surface appearance to be confused with underlying reality (the practice later to be condemned as 'naivety' in literary modernism). Lukács' withdrawal from active political life is symptomatic of deep-seated problems within Marxist theory itself, which were never really to be resolved. From the beginning of his career as a Marxist Lukács is to be found insisting that political correctness is no guarantee of the truth of your particular analysis of reality. If process is not taken into account, your analysis is at best worthless, at worst pernicious; without process there is to be the long decline into 'habit, convention and routine, none of which are able to adapt themselves to the demands of the moment' ('The Question of Parliamentarianism', p. 54).

Lukács' tactical flexibility, his constant striving to match tactics to historical process, can be seen to particular advantage when we counterpose 'The Question of Parliamentarianism' to the 'Blum Theses'. Eight years separate the two pieces, the former being written in 1920, the latter in 1928. Parliamentarianism, that is, participation in the democratic electoral process, was a hotly debated issue of the time in communist circles. Lukács comes out strongly against the procedure in 1920, arguing that such cooperation with bourgeois institutions runs the risk of diluting socialist consciousness and deflecting the party from its long-term objective of overcoming bourgeois democracy. 'Even the most severe criticism levelled *within* that framework changes absolutely nothing,' he complains of communist parliamentary participation, adding:

> On the contrary: the very fact that severe criticism of bourgeois society appears *possible* within the confines of parliament serves, just as the bourgeoisie would wish it, to confuse the class-consciousness of the proletariat. Indeed the myth of bourgeois parliamentary democracy depends precisely on the ability of parliament to appear not as an organ of class oppression, but as the organ of the 'entire people'. (*Ibid.*, p. 57)

The clear message is that to enter parliament at all, even with the stated objective of bringing about its ultimate dissolution, is to jeopardise one's revolutionary credibility. The institution that the communist deputy enters is not ideologically neutral but part of the repressive mechanism of the state: participation therefore equals collusion. In the heady atmosphere of 1920, with the old social order in a state of considerable disarray and revolutionary hopes running high in the Marxist camp, such sentiments are understandable enough, although they are shortly to be attacked by the more sober-minded Lenin in his essay '"Left-wing" communism – an infantile disorder'. The Lukácsian position on parliamentarianism was part of the 'left-wing' deviation in Lenin's view: 'G. L.'s article is very Left-wing and very poor,' he complains. 'Its Marxism is purely verbal.'[3]

One of Lukács' great worries about parliamentary participation is that it will create a rift, not just between the party and the proletariat, but between the parliamentary faction and the party: 'experience has taught us that the relationship between party and parliamentary faction is almost always inverted, with the party being pulled in the wake of the parliamentary faction' (*Ibid.*, p. 61). The old Marxist fear of an elite which will start to see reality in its own image, according to its own self-interested concerns, emerges. Lukács' answer to the problem, in line with his belief in the proletariat's historic mission, is the workers' council, an institution completely untainted by bourgeois principles. As he was to remark later in his study on Lenin, it is in the nature of workers' soviets to be 'an anti-government' (*LSUT*, p. 69), therefore they are always to be encouraged.

'Blum Theses'

Lukács' arguments are sound enough in their way, although they are open to criticism on the grounds that they misread the level of socialist consciousness actually achieved at the time of writing. Thus in Lenin's verdict, 'The Question of Parliamentarianism' 'gives no concrete analysis of precise and definite historical situations; it takes no account of what is most essential (the need to take over and to learn to take over, all fields of work and all institutions in which the bourgeoisie exerts its influence over the masses, etc.)'.[4] To Lukács' credit he realises this over the course of the 1920s and, taking Lenin's criticisms to heart, modifies his position in a show of tactical flexibility. It is one thing to be critical of the parliamentarian route in the highly promising social situation of 1920, another thing altogether still to be doing so in the darker days of 1928 with several years of setbacks for communism to reflect upon and fascism on the rise throughout Europe, and the 'Blum Theses' accordingly adopt a different line on the issue. The 'Blum Theses' argue the case for a democratic transition to communism in Hungary given the special circumstances of the Hungarian situation: its economic backwardness, predominantly peasant population, and the nature of the right-wing regime currently in power. After extensive discussion within the HCP the 'Blum Theses' were rejected, Lukács was accused of rightist deviation, threatened with expulsion, and his active political career, despite a tactical recantation on his part of the 'Blum Theses', was for the time being at an end.

The 'Blum Theses' constitute a very sober assessment of the political situation facing the HCP in the late 1920s. A right-wing government is apparently firmly entrenched, and dictatorship of the proletariat is not imminent. Given these generally unpromising circumstances Lukács calls for the party to work towards a 'democratic dictatorship' of the proletariat and the peasantry, arguing the urgent necessity of extending the class struggle beyond the boundaries of the proletariat. Lukács is at pains to assure the party that democratic dictatorship will not be an end in itself but rather a stage in a continuing dialectical process:

> To stop at democratic dictatorship, conceived as a fixed, 'constitutionally determined' period of development, would necessarily signify the victory of the counter-revolution. Democratic dictatorship can therefore be understood only as the concrete transition by means of which the bourgeois revolution turns into the revolution of the proletariat. 'There is no Chinese wall between bourgeois revolution and the revolution of the proletariat' (Lenin).   ('Blum Theses', 1928–9', p. 243)

Such arguments prove to no avail, however, and, not for the last time in Lukács' career, the dogmatists are to win.

Lukács' tactical flexibility, while certainly admirable on a personal level, is also indicative of a problem within Marxist theory itself: the problem of matching the theory to concrete socio-political reality with any consistent hope of success. So often over the course of these writings, the 'Blum Theses' included, Lukács seems to be calling attention to mismatches of theory and practice, misinterpretations of the political situation, misreadings of public consciousness and spurious tactical decisions, that one begins to wonder about the efficacy of a theory that can lead its adherents into quite so much error. There are seemingly always adjustments to be made in the way that the theory is interpreted or applied until one despairs of anyone (except perhaps Lenin, whom Lukács consistently praises) ever getting the equation quite right. Flexibility almost becomes part of the problem since the theory shows itself capable of yielding so many conflicting interpretations of given situations. It is perhaps not so surprising that there was a tendency for the dialectical subtlety of a Lukács to be replaced by a party-centred dogmatism.

'Tribune or Bureaucrat?'

The rejection of the 'Blum Theses' was the signal for Lukács to devote more time to the study of literary realism, but politics, in the guise of Stalinism, periodically intrudes. 'Tribune or Bureaucrat?' represents Lukács' first fully sustained engagement with the problem of Stalin, and in its tortuous arguments conjures up the repressiveness of the period nearly as effectively as a Solzhenitsyn narrative does. By 1940 the character of the Stalinist state – bureaucratic, dogmatic, repressive – was well established. 'Tribune or Bureaucrat?' is an attack on this phenomenon, which manages, or feels it prudent, to absolve Stalin of any personal blame for the development. Bureaucracy is described as a fundamental element of capitalist society, a weapon of the bourgeoisie in its struggle to maintain its ascendancy over other classes, and as such totally inimical to the whole idea of a socialist state. 'The mere existence of bureaucracy in a Soviet system', Lukács insists in uncompromising fashion, 'even if the individual bureaucrats are subjectively honest, objectively amounts to assistance to the hostile powers. . . . Bureaucracy is a foreign body under socialism' ('Tribune or Bureaucrat?', *ER*, p. 229). In another of his typical binary oppositions (borrowed this time from Lenin) Lukács pictures the socialist state as resolving into a choice between two types of public official, the bureaucrat or the people's tribune, the latter being, in Lenin's words, someone

> who is able to react to every manifestation of tyranny and oppression, no matter where it appears, no matter what stratum or class of the people it affects . . . who is able to take advantage of every event, however small, in order to set forth *before all* his socialist convictions and his democratic demands, in order to clarify for *all* and everyone the world-historic significance of the struggle for the emancipation of the proletariat.[5]

The bureaucrat, on the other hand, is a person who has effectively surrendered himself to the smooth running of the bureaucratic mechanism, who functions purely as a cog in a machine and even takes pride in so doing. Such specialisation of task, a typical consequence of capitalism's division of labour principle, has the effect of disguising from the individual the larger process that is taking place. The bureaucrat can no longer see this wider picture, he 'lives within a world of forms with apparent laws of its own' (p. 233). Bureaucratic specialisation is, therefore, part of the mystification of process that a confirmed dialectical thinker like Lukács must always oppose wherever he finds it (in modernist literature and philosophy no less than in political systems).[6] Bureaucracy militates against the critical temper of dialectical thought.

Comrade Stalin, however, is not to be implicated in such un-socialist practices, and is portrayed as the sworn enemy of bureaucracy:

> Both Lenin and Stalin viewed the perpetuation of bureaucracy as a damaging inheritance of capitalism, as well as an inheritance of the particular economic and cultural backwardness of prerevolutionary Russia. The abolition of bureaucracy thus forms part of the Stalinist programme for liquidating the economic and ideological survivals of capitalist society.   (p. 228)

It is difficult to know how to take that last sentence, for Stalin was the architect of the bureaucracy that Lukács is calling into question, and Lukács well knew that by 1940 after being resident in Moscow for several years. (He was to claim repeatedly in later life that he was an opponent of Stalinist ideas in the 1930s and 1940s.) Indeed, his essay is ironic proof of how deeply the bureaucracy is entrenched in that he feels unable to criticise its chief begetter and beneficiary.

Perhaps one can be too critical here; opposition to Stalin after the purges of the mid-1930s (which Lukács witnessed at first hand) was hardly feasible, and from that point of view Lukács is simply protecting himself – something for which he cannot reasonably be blamed. What is more difficult to decide is just how much of a veiled attack on Stalin the essay is overall. Stalin himself was making anti-bureaucratic noises, while in reality operating in a highly bureaucratic manner, so he is unlikely to have been especially concerned by Lukács' line of argument. While it is unrealistic to expect everyone to make heroic gestures under a tyranny as extreme as Stalin's, a question-mark nevertheless hangs over Lukács' anti-Stalinism, which 'Tribune or Bureaucrat?' fails to dispel. It is just as possible to argue that the essay contributes to the personality cult as that it opposes it, and that ambivalence makes it hard to assess the extent to which Lukács really was a source of an alternative view of Marxism in the period. In a late interview Lukács is to be found arguing that 'Anyone who reads my articles from the 1920s and 30s will see that even at that time I was in disagreement with Stalin's and Zhdanov's line' (*MHL*, p. 314), but 'Tribune or Bureaucrat?' gives one some pause on the matter.

Anti-Stalinism

After Stalin's death in 1953, however, Lukács soon became one of the bitterest critics of the Stalinist legacy in the Eastern bloc. 'Reflections on the Cult of Stalin' (1962) is a good example of his open anti-Stalinism with its identification of 'sectarianism', the deliberate suppression of intermediate factors in the analysis of a problem, as the distinguishing characteristic of Stalinist method: 'the Stalinist tendency is always to abolish, wherever possible, all intermediate factors, and to establish an immediate connection between the crudest factual data and the most general theoretical propositions' (*MHL*, p. 66). This is an acute analysis, although it coexists rather uneasily with the 'Stalin as the scourge of the bureaucrats' line of 'Tribune or Bureaucrat?' Stalin is seen to be an essentially undialectical thinker, one of the worst sins that a Marxist can be guilty of as far as a subtle dialectician like Lukács is concerned, and compared unfavourably to Lenin. A sociological explanation is offered for Stalinism which directs our attention to the apparatus which produced and sustained the cult of personality:

> I pictured Stalin to myself as the apex of a pyramid which widened gradually toward the base and was composed of many 'little Stalins': they, seen from above, were the objects and, seen from below, the creators and guardians of the 'cult of the personality'.   (p. 62)

Again, this is an acute analysis and a noteworthy one for eschewing the easy option of simply blaming Stalinism on Stalin's own personality, which would represent an unacceptable lapse into the 'great men' approach to history for a Marxist. It does not, however, pursue this line of thought as far as it might, say into the question of whether there is not something within Marxism itself that is conducive to the production of Stalin pyramids. Rather lamely, Lukács' sociological analysis settles for citing several historical factors – Russia's relative cultural backwardness, war devastation, foreign military interventions, Lenin's struggle within his own party – as likely culprits; all very true, no doubt, but not the whole story surely for the proliferation of 'little Stalins' over so long a period. The dialectical probing can only go so far into the theory itself.

Stalinism is also the target in 'Reflections on the Sino-Soviet Dispute' (1963), where Chinese communism is included in the sectarian heresy. Both Stalinists and Chinese communists, Lukács maintains, 'manifest a sovereign manipulation of facts while offering Marxist-Leninist certification for the most capricious bureaucratic actions' (*MHL*, p. 81), and he speaks of the Chinese as having taken over 'the formally closed pseudotheoretical style of the Stalin period' (p. 73). Lukács is scathing of what he considers to be the Chinese regime's Stalinist-like reliance on propagandistic catchphrases at the expense of dialectical argument. It is yet another chapter in the long-running story of Lukács versus the dogmatists, and it shows Lukács to be as concerned as ever with the need to match one's theories to the actual reality of historical process. Catchphrases persisted in for their own sake, the Chinese–Stalinist tactic, merely proclaim the presence of a divorce between theory and reality.

The political writings reveal Lukács to be a consistent enemy of vulgar Marxism in whatever guise it chooses to present itself, a subtle dialectician and tactician, and a scourge of the dogmatist mentality. But what he never succeeds in doing is problematising the basic theory itself to discover why it is so prone to generating deviations and lapses from the path of dialectical virtue. The one thing that Lukács himself remains dogmatic about is the truth of Marxist theory, and in the late interview referred to earlier, we can observe the limits of his dialectical flexibility being staunchly maintained to the end:

> For Marxism, just as much as everything else, falls under the rule that there is only one truth. History is either the history of class struggle or it is not . . . . We must be clear about the fact that in every issue there is only one truth and that we Marxists are struggling for its emergence. (*MHL*, p. 326)

CHAPTER
EIGHT

Lukács' critical legacy:
Goldmann and Jameson

Lukács' long tenure as a Marxist theorist – more than half a century of high-profile activity – means that his influence is widely diffused throughout contemporary critical discourse. Often this is in indirect ways: *HCC*, as we have noted, provided a source of inspiration for the Frankfurt School and Walter Benjamin, whose aesthetic theories in turn were absorbed and adapted by later generations of theorists to help form current critical debates. We have noted too the echoes of Lukács in structural Marxism and 'reading against the grain' technique. To a certain extent all Marxist literary theorists have to position themselves with regard to Lukács (particularly over the issue of realism), but in terms of direct rather than indirect influence Lukács' leading disciple has been the Franco-Romanian critic, Lucien Goldmann (1913–70). After Goldmann, Lukács' critical legacy is at its most powerful in the work of the American critic Fredric Jameson, a consistent admirer of the Lukácsian approach to aesthetic and cultural enquiry. The critical methods of these two figures will be considered briefly to give a taste – if no more than that – of Lukács' impact on later twentieth-century critical discourse.[1]

Lucien Goldmann

Goldmann was most influenced by Lukács' earlier writings, up to and including *HCC*, and his sociology of literature draws heavily on this period of Lukács' career. Indeed Goldmann identifies *TN* as the source for his theory of 'genetic structuralism', which seeks to establish homologies, or structural parallels, between literary texts and the world-views of certain social groups contemporary with he texts; thus in *The Hidden God* Goldmann postulates parallels between the tragic vision in Pascal's philosophy and Racine's plays, and that informing extreme Jansenism (a controversial movement within the Catholic Church of the time). The great writer for Goldmann is one who 'achieves a coherent awareness of what, among the other members of his group, remains vague and confused, and contradicted by innumerable other tendencies',[2] and this is what both Pascal and Racine proceed to do in the articulation of their tragic vision. There are resonances here of Lukács' idea, expressed in *SF*, that literature gives form to the chaos around us in everyday life, and perhaps even of the theory of realism with its belief that the greatest literature is that which succeeds in reflecting the essential nature of reality to an audience which is struggling with reification in its various, reality obscuring forms. Texts are to be seen as expressions of group, or class, consciousness. Crucially, the world visions of such groups or classes are not static but in dialectical interaction with their world: 'Thus human realities are presented as two–sided processes: *destructuration* of old structurations and *structuration* of new totalities capable of creating equilibria capable of satisfying the new demands of the social groups that are elaborating them.'[3] Texts are heavily implicated in this complex dialectical process of destructuration and structuration.

Goldmann's *Towards a Sociology of the Novel* takes its lead from *TN*, with some help from René Girard's *Mensonge romantique et vérité romanesque* (1961). The concern is to construct a sociology of the novel, which will explain the relation between novel form and the structure of the social environment in which the form was created. Goldmann insists upon a close connection, arguing that it is inconceivable that a form of such dialectical complexity as the novel should have developed over time in so many different social contexts without there being any homology at all between it and the most significant aspects of social existence. That there is such a rigorous homology is the working hypothesis of the study which goes on to examine how this operates in the novels of André Malraux. The novel develops as a genre within a social context, that of capitalism, in which individuals are subject to the dehumanising effects of commodity fetishism and the reification that accompanies it: 'the *evolution* of the fictional form that corresponds to the world of reification can be understood only in so far as it is related to a *homologous history* of the structure of reification.'[4] Goldmann draws Marxist conclusions from *TN*: the lost and lonely individual of the latter is lost and lonely as a direct result of capitalism's distortion of human relations to fit the needs of the market. The literary form emerges from an economic reality.

Genetic structuralism concerns itself with the relations between part and whole in social totalities; thus the relation between an important work of art and the social group which, as Goldmann puts it, '*is in the last resort, the true subject of creation*',[5] is equivalent to that between specific elements of the work and the work itself as a whole. The genetic structuralist method has the twin task of outlining the precise nature of the relations between work and group, and of establishing which works and groups may be so related. The firm commitment to totality that marks out Lukács' work finds a response in Goldmann, who sees genetic structuralist research as consisting of 'the fact of delimiting groups of empirical data that constitute structures, relative totalities, in which they can later be inserted as elements in other larger, but similar structures'.[6] Such a method of analysis is considered to be both comprehensive and explanatory, as in the case of Goldmann's researches in *The Hidden God*, where

to elucidate the tragic structure of Pascal's *Pensées* and Racine's tragedies is a process of comprehension; to insert them into extremist Jansenism by uncovering the structure of this school of thought is a process of comprehension in relation to the latter, but a process of explanation in relation to the writings of Pascal and Racine; to insert extreme Jansenism into the overall history of Jansenism is to explain the first and to understand the second. To insert Jansenism, as a movement of ideological expression, into the history of the seventeenth-century *noblesse de robe* is to explain Jansenism and to understand the *noblesse de robe*. To insert the history of the *noblesse de robe* into the overall history of French society is to explain it by understanding the latter, and so on.[7]

Genetic structuralism reveals itself to be an historically conscious exercise in mapping the complex dialectical processes involved in the production of texts. Just how complex is evident when we come to consider extreme Jansenism and the texts it helps to generate. A reactionary movement within seventeenth-century French society (the bourgeoisie being the progressive historical force of the time and Cartesian rationalism its ideological manifestation), Jansenism can be regarded as progressive in the longer term in that it represents a challenge to Cartesian rationalism and a significant step on the road to dialectical thinking. Like Lukács his model, Goldmann is not deterred by a reactionary exterior and can find progressive potential in apparently unpromising (from a Marxist perspective) texts and authors.

Behind genetic structuralism lies the same kind of desire to grasp the totality of historical process that had motivated Lukács, and Lukács' own early career becomes a subject for genetic structuralist research in another of Goldmann's studies, *Lukács and Heidegger: Towards a new philosophy*, where homologies are sought between these two philosophers up to the date of the writing of Heidegger's *Being and Time*.[8] It is not just a case, as Goldmann claims it is in standard sociological surveys, of trying to locate the genesis of a work (most likely in some aspect of the author's life, a consideration of no more importance to Goldmann than it was to Lukács), but of contextualising the structural parallels between work and group in the widest possible, dialectically conceived, historical framework.

The structural study of Malraux's novels that goes to make up the bulk of *Towards a Sociology* explores the homologies that exist between that author's fiction and the turbulent period of European history within which it was written. Goldmann posits three broad periods in the history of Western capitalism: the expansion-minded liberal capitalism of the later nineteenth and earlier twentieth centuries; the capitalism in structural crisis between roughly 1912 and 1945; and the advanced state-regulated capitalism of the post-Second World War world. Malraux's ideological development is taken to be an expression of the change consequent on the shift from the second to the third period. Goldmann argues that the internal coherence he finds in Malraux's works suggests that he is a particularly representative writer, whose 'development poses, in the double sense of its nature and of the dangers that it contains, the principal problems raised by the relations between culture and the most recent phase in the history of Western industrial societies'.[9] There is, in other words, a homology to be noted between Malraux's intellectual trajectory, his sensitivity to the intellectual and moral crises of the Western world, and the course of Western capitalism.

In general terms of reference the homology that we are to look out for in the twentieth century is that between the rise of monopoly capitalism (a development occurring at the end of the liberal capitalist period) and the dissolution and disappearance of the hero figure in the novel. Goldmann suggests that from Kafka onwards what we tend to observe in the development of the novel form is 'an abandonment of any attempt to replace the problematic hero and individual biography by another reality and by the effort to write the novel of the absence of the subject',[10] which, if it seems to exclude from consideration both the critical realist and socialist realist traditions, at least offers us a less judgemental way of approaching Kafka and the modernists than Lukács does.

Fredric Jameson

Goldmann's debt to Lukács is clear, and regularly acknowledged by him. In Jameson there is a debt too and no lack of approving references to Lukács' project to be noted over the course of the former's *oeuvre* (Jameson also remarks approvingly on 'the historic and indeed incomparable role played by Lucien Goldmann in the reawakening of Marxist theory in contemporary France').[11] Jameson has struggled to keep a Lukács-inspired Hegelian–Marxist tradition alive in American academic culture in the face of stiff competition from, successively, Althusserian structuralism, poststructuralism and postmodernism. Admitting the rampant pluralism of today's intellectual marketplace, Jameson sets out to argue the case for Marxism, conceiving of the theory as 'that "untranscendable horizon" that subsumes such apparently antagonistic or incommensurable critical operations'.[12] Jameson's is an unashamed defence of Marxism as meta-narrative, which meets the postmodernist challenge of Lyotard *et al.* head on. The Lukácsian–Hegelian–Marxist belief in the dialectic as the key to unlocking the narrative of history survives intact in Jameson, for whom postmodernism reveals itself to be 'the cultural logic of late capitalism'[13] – in effect, another instance of the 'indirect apologetics' Lukács was always at such pains to identify throughout his Marxist critical writings.

Jameson's defence of Lukács' project in *Marxism and Form* ('The Case for Georg Lukács') is worth dwelling on for a moment to see where he locates Lukács' strengths. Jameson has a totalising approach to Lukács' career, which he interprets as

> a progressive exploration and enlargement of a single complex of problems . . . a continuous lifelong meditation on narrative, on its basic structures, its relationship to the reality it expresses, and its epistemological value when compared with other, more abstract and philosophical modes of understanding.[14]

The virtue of *TN* is that it conceives of the novel as a modern attempt to reconcile matter and spirit, life and essence, which, because of the unfavourable conditions of the modern world, is inherently problematical in its structure, a form requiring continual reinvention in response to events. What Lukács' enquiry discloses is that in order for the novel to become epic again there will have to be a radical transformation of society and the world in which he lives. The perceived weaknesses of *TN* – the 'golden age' nostalgia, the strained typology, the over-metaphysical conception of human existence – cannot for Jameson detract from its very real merit in isolating what is missing in modern life. It is a lack which will be made good in Lukács' own case by Marxism, which provides him with the method to make sense of the modern world's disjointed narrative. In *HCC* Marxism enables Lukács to identify those forces within the present (proletarian class consciousness, for example) that can overcome reification and dispel the air of despair hanging over *TN*. *HCC* amounts to a 'humiliation of middle-class philosophy',[15] which sets the stage for Lukács' subsequent exploration of those works which have been most successful in reflecting social reality in all its concrete historicity – that is, the great realism of the nineteenth century and its twentieth-century critical realist equivalent.

While Jameson admires Lukács' reading of the great realists, he finds the reading of modernism, which turns out to be a case of both 'diagnosis and judgement' on Lukács' part,[16] more questionable, although even here he feels that Lukács' perspective as an outsider permits him to recognise the nature of the ideology governing modernism with a greater sense of clarity than those theorists caught up inside the phenomenon. It is not so much the diagnosis that Jameson disapproves of, as the judgement that accompanies it, since such a judgement 'presupposes that the modernist writer has some personal choice in the matter, and that his fate is not sealed for him by the logic of his moment in history'.[17] Take away that presupposition and the diagnosis of modernism is still eminently defensible.

Overall Lukács is to be valued, Jameson contends, for his insistence on the relationship between narrative and totality (and for 'narrative' we can also read 'process'), and Jameson is no less a believer in the Lukácsian vision of totality than Goldmann was before him, nor of it being the critical duty to trace historical process in all its dialectical complexity. Lukács' critical heritage hinges precisely on commitment to those two elements, narrative process and totality, and in the critical methods of Goldmann and Jameson we find that commitment being faithfully honoured.

Conclusion

Several unresolved problems remain at the end of this survey. First, there is the issue of realism. Lukács' defence of literary realism can be very persuasive within its own terms of reference and he provides an interesting new perspective from which to view the novels of the great realists of the nineteenth century. However, doubts still persist as to the validity of the theory in general, especially when it is used as a stick with which to beat modernism. One suspects that Lukács' personal preferences are driving the theory far more than ideally they should, and that to a large extent these preferences are rooted in the past. There is nothing wrong with this until the past changes from being a personal preference to being a model, and that is a line Lukács is guilty of crossing. Realism then turns into a fetish, a transformation that is inimical to a creative art which can only too easily ossify if tied to the practices of the past. Brecht's weary recitation of the Lukácsian realist formula – 'writers must simply retain the old patterns, produce a rich life of the spirit, hold back the pace of events by a slow narrative, advance the individual to the centre of the stage by their art, and so on'[1] – suggests just how dreary a prospect it could be to artists seeking to challenge their audience's cosy assumptions about the world around them. Lukács cannot so much offer a definition of realism as point to a series of works that he likes

(Scott, Balzac, Tolstoy, Mann, those names that keep recurring) and call that realism. That would be the most honest answer to Anna Seghers' request that Lukács 'again define exactly what you mean by realism', and it is a less than satisfactory one from a theoretical standpoint: something much harder-edged is required as the basis for an aesthetic theory than a set of personal likes and dislikes. Time flows on, as Brecht points out, but in a very real sense Lukács' aesthetic understanding does not, and he has to bear his share of responsibility for realism's somewhat Stalinist effect – every criticism a threat as Brecht complained – within the field of Marxist aesthetics.

Lukács provides no final answer to the phenomenon of Stalinism either, and many unanswered questions linger at both the personal and theoretical level: How taken in was he by Stalinism in the 1930s and 1940s? How opportunist is he in jumping on the anti-Stalinist bandwagon after Stalin's death? Does the theory of the vanguard role of the party, which both Lukács and Lenin hold, merely succeed in paving the way for a Stalinist-style tyranny? Even more to the point, is Stalinism a natural consequence of Marxist theory in general? When quizzed on the latter possibility by an interviewer near the end of his life, Lukács is evasive and unconvincing in his reply: 'If I say to you that two times two is four and you as my orthodox follower insist that the answer is six, then I am not responsible for that' (*RL*, p. 101). This may be true, but it does not address the issue of why orthodoxy would wish to make such an outrageous claim, or what historical processes lie behind its wish. Neither does it face up to the issue of the responsibility that everyone surely shares for allowing orthodoxy to enforce compliance with such patently ridiculous claims. Lukács has no very satisfactory explanation of how Stalinism came to be the system that could both claim that two plus two was six and ensure its acceptance as dogma. Insisting that Marxism is a method and not a body of doctrine is all very well, but it has revealed an unfortunate tendency to produce dogmatists of the Stalinist variety (first the Russian originals and then the Chinese-Stalinists Lukács so abhorred in later life), and something has to account for the development and durability of the Stalin pyramid within a Marxist society. One might complain that no truly dialectical explanation of Stalinism is ever offered in the pages of Lukács, and perhaps that is a significant omission since such an explanation may well run the risk of undermining the basic theory to which Lukács is committed.

Lukács' sharp dividing line between reason and unreason also begs several questions. Once again one suspects that personal preference plays rather a large part: also that some scores are being settled with the author's youth. It is almost as if Nietzsche has come to represent everything that Lukács despises about his non-Marxist past and must be castigated accordingly. The possibility that works may shift back and forward between reason and unreason depending on the state of play politically and theoretically – as has happened with Nietzsche's *oeuvre* over the years – is one that Lukács fails to allow for; indeed, he seems to be arguing that there is some core of reason or unreason in all works of literature or philosophy which has a highly predictable impact on consciousness. The essentialist in Lukács is to the fore at such points, and one might wish to take issue with his totalising tendencies and argue that the categories of reason and unreason are in fact much more fluid than he desires them to be. Deconstruction would certainly want to tease apart this loaded binary opposition with its belief in stable and uncontaminated signs. In effect, reason and unreason amount to moral judgements on Lukács' part, and his aesthetic theory can be criticised as being over-dependent on such disguised judgements.

If unresolved problems persist in Lukács' concepts of realism, reason and unreason, as well as in the exact nature of his relationship to Stalinism, there are still many positive things to note about his work that suggest he manages to transcend the Marxist moment. His critiques of reflection theory on the crude Plekhanov model and socialist realism's appropriation by the politicians for short-term political goals, indicates that Lukács was well aware of the weaknesses in Marxist aesthetics. Interestingly enough, he admitted in a late interview that one of the things that attracted him to Stalin in the late 1920s and early 1930s was that the latter was highly critical of Plekhanov, whose concept of aesthetic value, as we have seen, assumed a very mechanistic relationship between art and ideology where the art of a politically decadent society could not itself escape being decadent also.[2] Reflection theory in Lukács' hands becomes a much more sophisticated, much more convincing way of explaining art's relationship to reality, which takes a significant step away from determinism and the concept of the artist as a passive medium through which outside forces work their will. 'If art reflects life', Brecht writes, 'it does so with special mirrors.'[3] On this at least the two adversaries could agree, the aesthetic being for Lukács very much a special category. Lukács is also just as harsh as any bourgeois critic on socialist realism, with its often wildly improbable picture of the brave new world of Stalinist socialism. The cruder forms of socialist realism always incur Lukács' displeasure, and inasmuch as it was the official aesthetic of the Stalinist regime his claim to have been anti-Stalinist during the regime's heyday has some substance, even if it does have to be balanced against other, less favourable behaviour on the author's part from the same period. Lukács is also to be commended for keeping up a dialogue with bourgeois literature at a time when it was only too tempting for the Marxist critic to write off such literature for political reasons. The critique of modernism notwithstanding, there is a degree of openness about Lukács as a critic that is unusual for the milieu in which he was working, a willingness to search for signs of dialectical awareness and historical change in the writings of his ideological adversaries.

Modernism is, however, the sticking point when it comes to Lukács' critical *oeuvre*, and there is no doubt that he is overzealous in consigning so many major twentieth-century authors to oblivion on the basis of their anti-realism and experimental bent. Yet anti-modernism can now be seen from another perspective – that of the postmodern. Experimentalism and inaccessibility are no longer in vogue, aesthetically speaking, and Lukács' anti-modernism looks less eccentric than it once did now that postmodernism has set about problematising the modernist aesthetic in earnest.

Postmodernism is an amorphous term, which covers a multitude of theoretical perspectives, but at least in some versions of it a sense of dialogue with the past is demanded. The architecture theorist Charles Jencks has been an eloquent advocate of such a procedure in his theory of double coding:

> I would define postmodernism . . . as double coding – the combination of modern techniques with something else (usually traditional building) in order for architecture to communicate with the public and a concerned minority, usually other architects . . . . The point of this double coding was itself double. Modern architecture had failed to

remain credible partly because it didn't communicate effectively with its ultimate users . . . and partly because it didn't make effective links with the city and history.[4]

Jencks even provides a Hegelian gloss on this duality of post-modernism, calling it 'the continuation of modernism and its transcendence',[5] which is effectively to see it as the sublation of the modernist aesthetic. Postmodernism is for Jencks a representational art, metaphorically oriented and historically conscious, and it constitutes an attempt to reintegrate the present with the past. Jencks speaks of a 'return to the larger Western tradition', noting that the trend has a variety of causes, 'but among the most important is the idea that the value of any work must depend partly on tradition, both for its placement and quality'.[6] Modernism is considered to be a failed project as far as the general public is concerned, an art-form designed for the elite that has lost sight of its social duty, and, indeed, of objective social reality.

Although there are important differences, which I will come to in a moment, much of what Jencks stands for recalls Lukács, who can easily be encompassed within an aesthetic programme that emphasises representationalism, historical consciousness, dialogue with the past and art's social role. The hermetic quality of modernism that Lukács was so critical of in *MCR* seems no more acceptable to Jencks, who is calling for an art that visibly engages with the objective world. The differences concern Jencks' opening up of the practice of double coding to attitudes such as irony, which, although it would find an echo in *TN*, would have a more problematical place in Lukács' scheme of realism. Umberto Eco is cited in irony's defence, suggesting that it can involve an affectionate playing with the discourse of the past:

> I think of the postmodern attitude as that of a man who loves a very cultivated woman and knows he cannot say to her 'I love you madly,' because he knows that she knows (and that she knows that he knows) that these words have already been written by Barbara Cartland. Still, there is a solution. He can say, 'As Barbara Cartland would put it, I love you madly.' . . . If the woman goes along with this, she will have received a declaration of love all the same. Neither of the two speakers will feel innocent, both will have accepted the challenge of the past, of the already said, which cannot be eliminated, both will consciously and with pleasure play the game of irony.[7]

It is unlikely that game-playing of this nature would have much appeal for Lukács, who at all times demands an attitude of moral seriousness in the construction of narrative, but nevertheless a sense of historical process has been reintroduced on the cultural agenda by the postmodernists in such a way as to open the door for a renewed dialogue with realism. One can certainly say of Lukács that he is fully alive to 'the challenge of the past' and always strives to keep Marxism in dialogue with it. The differences should not be allowed to obscure a very real community of interest between postmodernist and critical realist aesthetics.

Postmodernism can also mean taking a much more sceptical attitude towards the past, as in the case of Lyotard and his problematising of 'grand narratives' such as Marxism: 'The grand narrative has lost its credibility, regardless of what mode of unification it uses . . . we can resort neither to the dialectic of Spirit nor even to the emancipation of humanity as a validation for postmodern scientific discourse.'[8] Lyotard's line of argument is anti-foundationalist and anti-authoritarian, and he is denying the ability of a theory like Marxism to ground a discourse or to serve as an unchallengeable authority and source of legitimation for political action.[9] All of this may make his brand of postmodernism sound a long way removed from the concerns of a Marxist like Lukács, but the latter's commitment to Marxism as a method rather than a body of doctrine has a postmodern ring to it all the same. As envisaged by Lukács, the method undercuts the grand narrative that builds up around doctrine where such figures as Engels are elevated to all but sacred status. Lukács is no more interested in a dogmatic grand narrative than Lyotard is – it suggests that its adherents are losing touch with objective reality, as was the case with Stalinists. Lukács' focus is always fixed on process. True, Lyotard explicitly questions the credibility of the dialectic, but it is the teleological Hegelian 'dialectic of the Spirit' that he singles out for condemnation in *The Postmodern Condition* and Lukács is no more enamoured of teleology than any anti-grand narrative theorist is. It is possible to make a case for the Marxist dialectic as anti-foundational since it is constantly in a process of unfolding, which militates – or at least ought to militate – against the construction of fixed grand narratives. The fairly purist conception of the dialectical method that we find in *HCC*, and that Lukács never really renounced despite all his recantations, has something of the iconoclasm of Lyotardean postmodernism. If not a sceptic on the Lyotard scale, Lukács is at least suspicious of the tendency of theory to harden into dogma.

This reading admittedly gives Lukács considerable benefit of the doubt since he became implicated to some extent in the creation of the grand narrative of Stalinism that proved so disastrous to the development of Marxism. Nevertheless it is important to register the anti-authoritarian possibilities of the dialectic if we are seeking to find out what can be retained from Lukács' work for a postmodern, post-Marxist age. It is to official Marxism's discredit that he was given so little scope to explore these possibilities at greater length, and that he was forced to spend so much of his career fending off the dogmatists. The concern with process certainly transcends the Marxist moment and aligns Lukács with Jencks-style postmodernism.

The question does arise as to whether Lukácsian realism is to be construed as a grand narrative, and it has to be admitted that it often seems to function much in that way. Lukács appears to conceive of realism in a similar manner to the dialectic, that is, as a method rather than a body of doctrine to be slavishly adhered to at all costs ('realism is not a style but the social basis of every truly great literature'), and the Solzhenitsyn study bears this out in being willing to countenance a departure from the standard form that realism has tended to adopt. Whether this is enough to deflect the grand narrative charge is another question. The parameters of realism in Lukácsian aesthetics are very tightly drawn, and the concept itself could only unequivocally move out of grand narrative territory if these parameters were loosened up quite considerably, perhaps on the lines suggested by Anna Seghers when she speculates 'whether there is any authentic work of art which does not contain a substance of realism, i.e. a tendency towards bringing reality into our consciousness'. Realism under this reading is simply equivalent to artistic method successfully executed, in which case the grand narrative charge falls away (unless of course 'authentic' proves to have hidden value commitments, at which point grand narrative sneaks back in). Lukács, as we know, is disinclined to accept such a loose formulation of realism; although one would have to say that in its absence, Marxist aesthetics finds it hard to avoid a divisive censoriousness and police-like mentality.

The source of the problem is the demand that the arts be judged in terms of their political effectiveness, which encourages the aesthetician to regard realism as the logical solution given its easy accessibility by the general public. What can be questioned is the assumption of an unproblematical link between aesthetic reception and political consciousness, which tends to reduce art to the status of glorified propaganda. Lukács' form of realism generally avoids such reductiveness, and he agrees that art-works affect us in complicated and often unpredictable ways, but even so he does assume causal links, no matter how complex in nature, between realism and authentic (that is, dialectically aware) consciousness, and modernism and false consciousness. We are left with a prescriptive aesthetics, and prescriptiveness is precisely where Marxist aesthetics is at its weakest and least attractive: the cultural police are soon out in force and they are rarely much disposed towards debate. Lukács' analyses of realist texts are perceptive up to the point where they become prescriptive: once past that point he is closer to the spirit of socialist realism than he would wish to be.

Take away the prescriptiveness and Lukács still has much to offer us as an aesthetician and cultural theorist. The strong sense of historical process and commitment to a dialogue with the past that mark out his work, and that represent Marxism at its best as a cultural theory, speak more clearly to a postmodernist than a modernist world. Lukács' conception of the dialectic indicates that Marxism need not be an authoritarian theory and that it can in fact have postmodern tendencies, although his career illustrates how difficult it could be to prevent the theory from internally generating a dogmatism that kept the anti-authoritarianism firmly in check. The victory of the dogmatists (which Lukács was to see at first hand in the Russia of the 1930s and the Hungary of the 1950s) meant that by the end of Lukács' career Marxism as a political force was living on borrowed time, but his work deserves to survive the collapse of Marxism in the West: realism is back on the agenda, so too is dialogue with the past, as is a generalised scepticism of doctrine-led political and social systems, and in each of these cases Lukács' writings have something important and thought-provoking to add to the debate.

Marxism's great success as an aesthetic theory has been to make us aware of art's ideological commitments and ideological role. The need for that awareness outlives Marxism's political decline –

feminism alone would be enough to prove the point, the rise of a culturally philistine right in Western politics would surely clinch it – and we should not forget Lukács' critical role in bringing about that condition of awareness. Perhaps what is needed now is for Lukács to be treated with the same kind of generosity that he extended towards the great realists of the nineteenth century: to acknowledge that, whatever ideological imperfections may exist in his work, he managed nevertheless to put the right kind of questions to his society.

Notes

Preface

1. See Jean-François Lyotard, *The Postmodern Condition: A report on knowledge*, translated by Geoff Bennington and Brian Massumi, Manchester: Manchester University Press, 1984.
2. See Perry Anderson, *Considerations on Western Marxism*, London: NLB, 1976, and *In the Tracks of Historical Materialism*, London: Verso, 1983; and Andrew Arato and Paul Brienes, *The Young Lukács and the Origins of Western Marxism*, New York: Seabury Press, 1979. Western Marxism is characterised by Anderson as academic and idealist, with a bias towards aesthetic and philosophical matters. While conceding such a bias, Arato and Brienes are more sympathetic to what they take to be the critical and humanistic temper of Western Marxism.
3. Fredric Jameson, *The Ideologies of Theory: Essays 1971–86*, Vol. I, London: Routledge, 1988, p. 57.

Historical and cultural context

1. For more on this generation, see Mary Gluck, *Georg Lukács and his Generation, 1900–18*, Cambridge, Mass.: Harvard University Press, 1985.
2. Quoted in Árpád Kadarkay, *Georg Lukács: Life, thought and politics*, Oxford and Cambridge, Mass.: Basil Blackwell, 1991, p. 56.
3. *Ibid.*, p. 25.
4. Georg Lukács, Preface, 1962, to *The Theory of the Novel: A historico-philosophical essay on the forms of great epic literature*, translated by Anna

Bostock, London: Merlin Press, 1971, p. 11. All further page references will be given in parentheses within the text.

5. Quoted in Kadarkay, *Georg Lukács*, p. 201. The Heidelberg connection was to plague Lukács for some time. Thus in 1939 we find the historian, Franz Borkenau, complaining of *History and Class Consciousness* that it was 'proclaimed in a vocabulary unintelligible not only to workingmen, but to any mortals who had not enjoyed a Heidelberg education' (Franz Borkenau, *World Communism: A history of the Communist International*, Ann Arbor, Mich.: University of Michigan Press, 1962, p. 174).

6. Georg Lukács, Preface, 1962, to *History and Class Consciousness: Studies in Marxist dialectics*, translated by Rodney Livingstone, London: Merlin Press, 1971, p. xxx. All further page references will be given in parentheses within the text.

7. *Soviet Writers' Congress 1934: The debate on socialist realism and modernism in the Soviet Union*, edited by H. G. Scott, London: Lawrence & Wishart, 1934, p. 21.

8. Georgi Plekhanov, *Art and Social Life*, translated by Eric Hartley and Eleanor Fox, London: Lawrence & Wishart, 1953, p. 223.

9. Georg Lukács, *Record of a Life: An autobiographical sketch*, translated by Rodney Livingstone, edited by István Eorsi, London: Verso, 1983, p. 95. All further page references will be given in parentheses within the text.

10. Terry Eagleton, *Criticism and Ideology: A study in Marxist literary theory*, London: NLB, 1976, p. 174.

11. Some scholars are in no doubt at all as to how to categorise Lukács on this issue: 'His case was one of genuine surrender to Stalinism, a surrender which was difficult and painful, yet voluntary and therefore in a sense irrevocable' (Isaac Deutscher, 'Georg Lukács and critical realism', *The Listener*, 3 November, 1966, pp. 659–62 (p. 659)).

12. See George Lichtheim, *Lukács*, London: Fontana/Collins, 1970. For another particularly critical reading of Lukács from the Cold War period, see Victor Zitta, *Georg Lukács' Marxism: Alienation, dialectics, revolution. A study in utopia and ideology*, The Hague: Martinus Nijhoff, 1964.

Chapter 1

1. Michael Lowy, *Georg Lukács – From Romanticism to Bolshevism*, translated by Patrick Camiller, London: NLB, 1979, p. 189.

2. Lukács' jaundiced view of the book's new readership can be gauged from his reply to an interviewer's observation that *HCC* had cult status among French students during the 1968 *événements*: 'Since the analysis of class consciousness contains idealist elements and since the ontological material of Marxism is therefore less in evidence than in my later works, the book is of course more accessible to bourgeois readers' (*RL*, pp. 77–8).

3. For more on the connections between Lukács and the Frankfurt School, see Andrew Feenberg, *Lukács, Marx and the Sources Of Critical Theory*, Oxford: Martin Robertson, 1981.

4. Later developed in more detail by Antonio Gramsci. See, for example, *Selections from the Prison Notebooks*, translated and edited by Quintin Hoare and Geoffrey Nowell Smith, London: Lawrence & Wishart, 1971.
5. George Lichtheim *Lukács*, London: Fontana/Collins, p. 67.
6. At the end of his life Lukács goes so far as to locate the roots of Stalinism in Engels' version of social determinism: 'after him [Engels] a number of Social Democrats, interpreted the idea of social determinism from a standpoint of logical necessity, as opposed to the actual social context of which Marx speaks' (*RL*, p. 105).
7. Immanuel Kant, *Critique of Pure Reason*, translated by Norman Kemp Smith, London and Basingstoke: Macmillan, 1933, p. 74.
8. Georg Lukács, *Marxism and Human Liberation: Essays on history, culture and revolution*, edited by E. San Juan Jr, New York: Dell Publishing, 1973, pp. 94, 85. All further page references will be given in parentheses within the text.
9. Feenberg, *Lukács, Marx*, p. 154.
10. Andrew Arato and Paul Brienes, *The Young Lukács and the Origins of Western Marxism*, New York: Seabury Press, 1979, p. 145.
11. Lichtheim, *Lukács*, p. 51.
12. Martin Jay, *Marxism and Totality: The adventures of a concept from Lukács to Habermas*, Cambridge and Oxford: Polity Press and Basil Blackwell, 1984, p. 113.
13. Georg Lukács, *Lenin: A study on the unity of his thought*, translated by Nicholas Jacobs, London: NLB, 1970, pp. 9, 12. All further page references will be given in parentheses within the text.
14. For more reflections on the connection between Prussian and fascist ideology, see Roy Pascal and D. M. Van Abbe, 'Prussianism and Nazism', *The Modern Quarterly*, 1/3 (1946), pp. 85–93, an adaptation of an article by Lukács published in the Soviet journal *International Literature*.
15. Georg Lukács, *The Young Hegel: Studies in the relations between dialectics and economics*, translated by Rodney Livingstone, London: Merlin Press, 1975, p. 50. All further page references will be given in parentheses within the text.
16. Lichtheim, *Lukács*, p. 108. Jean Hyppolite, on the other hand, is persuaded enough by Lukács' reading to suggest that perhaps Hegel is 'not as much of a theologian as one might be led to believe' (Jean Hyppolite, *Studies on Marx and Hegel*, translated by John O'Neill, London: Heinemann, 1969, p. 71).
17. Georg Lukács, *The Ontology of Social Being: 1. Hegel*, translated by David Fernbach, London: Merlin Press, 1978, pp. 61–2. All further page references will be given in parentheses within the text.
18. Georg Lukács, *The Ontology of Social Being: 2. Marx*, translated by David Fernbach, London: Merlin Press, 1978, p. 56. All further page references will be given in parentheses within the text.
19. Ferenc Fehér, Agnes Heller, György Markus and Mihály Vajda, 'Notes on Lukács' ontology', translated by David Parent, in Agnes Heller (ed.), *Lukács Revalued*, Oxford: Basil Blackwell, 1983, pp. 125–53 (p. 129).
20. 'I would prefer the *Destruction of Reason* as my first philosophical work in English rather than *Young Hegel*. I may be an optimist but it might create the same response as *The Historical Novel*' (Letter to István Mészaros, 10 May

1962; quoted in Árpád Kadarkay, *Georg Lukács: Life, thought and politics*, Oxford: Basil Blackwell, 1991, p. 422). In this case the optimism was very much misplaced.

21. *Encounter* (August, 1963), p. 95; H. A. Hodges, 'Lukács on irrationalism', in G. H. R. Parkinson (ed.), *Georg Lukács: The man, his work, and his ideas*, London: Weidenfeld & Nicolson, 1970, pp. 86–108 (p. 90); István Mészaros, *Lukács' Concept of Dialectic*, London: Merlin Press, 1972.
22. Georg Lukács, *The Destruction of Reason*, translated by Peter Palmer, London: Merlin Press, p. 85. All further page references will be given in parentheses within the text.
23. For just such an accusation, and Lukács' not very convincing reply to it, see the interview in *RL*, p. 101.

Chapter 2

1. For an alternative view on this, see J. M. Bernstein, *The Philosophy of the Novel: Lukács, Marxism and the dialectic of form*, Minneapolis: University of Minnesota Press, 1984, where it is argued that '*TN* is, as a matter of fact if not intention, a Marxist work; or rather, more precisely, a properly Marxist theory of the novel can be excavated from *TN*' (p. xii). Paul de Man is another to believe that the distinction between Lukács' early and later works can be overstated (see Paul de Man, *Blindness and Insight: Essays in the rhetoric of contemporary criticism*, London: Methuen, 1983, chapter 4).
2. Georg Lukács, *Soul and Form*, translated by Anna Bostock, London: Merlin Press, 1974, p. 153. All further page references will be given in parentheses within the text.
3. René Wellek, *Four Critics: Croce, Valéry, Lukács, and Ingarden*, Seattle and London: University of Washington Press, 1981, p. 38.
4. Jacques Derrida, *Writing and Difference*, translated by Alan Bass, Chicago: University of Chicago Press, 1978, p. 30.
5. Fredric Jameson, *Marxism and Form: Twentieth-century dialectical theories of literature*, Princeton, N.J.: Princeton University Press, 1971, p. 179.
6. *Ibid.*, p. 172.

Chapter 3

1. Georg Lukács, *Writer and Critic and Other Essays*, translated and edited by Arthur Kahn, London: Merlin Press, 1970, p. 111. All further page references will be given in parentheses within the text.
2. Peter Demetz, *Marx, Engels and the Poets*, translated by Jeffrey L. Sammons, Chicago and London: University of Chicago Press, 1967, p. 226.

Chapter 4

1. Georg Lukács, *Studies in European Realism: A sociological survey of the writings of Balzac, Stendhal, Zola, Tolstoy, Gorki and others*, translated by Edith Bone, London: Merlin Press, 1972, p. 139. All further page references will be given in parentheses within the text.
2. Pierre Machérey, *A Theory of Literary Production*, translated by Geoffrey Wall, London, Henley, and Boston: Routledge & Kegan Paul, 1978, p. 131.
3. István Mészaros, *Marx's Theory of Alienation*, 4th edition, London: Merlin Press, 1975, p. 195.
4. Georg Lukács, *Essays on Realism*, translated by David Fernbach, edited by Rodney Livingstone, London: Lawrence & Wishart, 1980, p, 235. All further page references will be given in parentheses within the text.
5. Georg Lukács, *The Historical Novel*, translated by Hannah and Stanley Mitchell, Harmondsworth: Penguin, 1969, pp. 9–10. All further page references will be given in parentheses within the text.
6. It is only fair to register that not everyone is persuaded by Lukács' evaluation of Scott. Roy Pascal, for example, claims that 'When we read Scott after reading Lukács, we are startled at the flatness of the writing, the complacency of the tone, at the lack of intensity, exaltation and anguish in our response' ('Georg Lukács: the concept of totality', in G.H.R. Parkinson (ed.), *Georg Lukács: The man, the work and his ideas*, London: Weidenfeld & Nicolson, 1970, pp. 147–71 (pp. 161–2)). Wellek too feels that Lukács 'grossly overrates Scott as an artist' (René Wellek, *Four Critics*, Seattle and London: University of Washington Press, 1981, p. 52).
7. Georg Lukács, *Goethe and his Age*, translated by Robert Anchor, London: Merlin Press, 1968, p. 149. All further page references will be given in parentheses within the text.

Chapter 5

1. Georg Lukács, *The Meaning of Contemporary Realism*, translated by John and Necke Mander, London: Merlin Press, 1963, p. 13. All further page references will be given in parentheses within the text.
2. Martin Heidegger, *Being and Time*, translated by John Macquarrie and Edward Robinson, London and New York: Basil Blackwell, 1962, pp. 174, 175.
3. Robert Musil, *The Man without Qualities*, Vol. I, translated by Eithne Wilkins and Ernst Kaiser, London: Picador, 1979, p. 85.
4. Georg Lukács, *Essays on Thomas Mann*, translated by Stanley Mitchell, London: Merlin Press, 1964, p. 163. All further page references will be given in parentheses within the text.
5. Peter Ackroyd's *Hawksmoor* is a notable example of what is now practically a sub-genre on its own.

6. Georg Lukács, *Solzhenitsyn*, translated by William David Graf, London: Merlin Press, 1970, p. 79. All further page references will be given in parentheses within the text.

Chapter 6

1. Bertolt Brecht, 'Against Lukács', translated by Stuart Hood, *New Left Review*, 84 (1974), pp. 33–53 (p. 51).
2. Walter Benjamin, *Understanding Brecht*, translated by Anna Bostock, London: NLB, 1973, p. 89.
3. Theodor W. Adorno, *Philosophy of Modern Music*, translated by Anne G. Mitchell and Wesley V. Bloomster, London: Sheed & Ward, 1973, p, 34.
4. Quoted in F. D. Klingender, *Marxism and Modern Art: An approach to social realism*, London: Lawrence & Wishart, 1943, p. 49.
5. Benjamin, *Understanding Brecht*, p. 116.
6. *Ibid.*, p. 118.
7. Brecht, 'Against Lukács', p. 45.
8. *Ibid.*, p. 50.
9. *Ibid.*, pp. 44–5.
10. *Ibid.*, p. 51.
11. *Ibid.*, p. 47.
12. *Ibid.*, p. 50.
13. *Ibid.*, p. 52. Terry Eagleton uses this as the basis for his own aesthetic theory of value in *Criticism and Ideology: A study in Marxist Literary Theory*, London: NLB, 1976: 'When Shakespeare's texts cease to make us think, they will cease to have value' (p. 169).
14. Stephen Eric Bronner, 'Between art and utopia: reconsidering the aesthetic theory of value of Herbert Marcuse', in Robert Pippin, Andrew Feenberg and Charles P. Webel (eds.), *Marcuse: Critical theory and the promise of utopia*, Basingstoke and London: Macmillan, 1988, pp. 107–40 (p. 130).

Chapter 7

1. Georg Lukács, *Political Writings 1919–1929: The question of parliamentarianism and other essays*, translated by Michael McColgan, edited by Rodney Livingstone, London: NLB, 1972. All further page references will be given in parentheses within the text.
2. For an excellent account of the various stages of Lukács's political thought in this period (from 'ultra-leftism' through 'political leftism' to 'left Bolshevism'), see Michael Lowy, *Georg Lukács – From Romanticism to Bolshevism*, translated by Patrick Camiller, London: NLB, 1979, chapter 3.
3. V. I. Lenin, *Collected Works*, vol. 31, London and Moscow, 1969–70: Lawrence & Wishart and Progress Publishers, p. 165.
4. *Ibid.*

5. Lenin, *Collected Works*, vol. 5, p. 243.
6. For a contrary view on this, see Cliff Slaughter, *Marxism, Ideology, and Literature*, London and Basingstoke: Macmillan, 1980, chapter 4, where it is argued that Lukács in fact reconciled himself to Soviet bureaucracy over the course of his life. Slaughter's Lukács is a somewhat devious character, at once a Stalinist and an unreconstructed bourgeois intellectual who has little real interest in the working class.

Chapter 8

1. For brief surveys of Goldmann's work see Cliff Slaughter, *Marxism, Ideology, and Literature*, London and Basingstoke: Macmillan, 1980 chapter 5, and Terry Eagleton, *Marxism and Literary Criticism*, London: Metheun, 1976; for Jameson, see Neil Larsen's Foreword to Fredric Jameson, *The Ideologies of Theory: Essays 1971–86*, London: Routledge, 1988.
2. Lucien Goldmann, *The Hidden God: A study of tragic vision in the 'Pensées' of Pascal and the tragedies of Racine*, translated by Philip Thody, London: Routledge & Kegan Paul, 1964, p. 315.
3. Lucien Goldmann, *Towards a Sociology of the Novel*, translated by Alan Sheridan, London: Tavistock, 1975, p. 156.
4. *Ibid.*
5. *Ibid.*, p. 158.
6. *Ibid.*, p. 162.
7. *Ibid.*, pp. 162–3.
8. Lucien Goldmann, *Lukács and Heidegger: Towards a new philosophy*, translated by William Q. Boelhower, London, Henley, and Boston: Routledge & Kegan Paul, 1977.
9. Goldmann, *Towards a Sociology*, p. 123.
10. *Ibid.*, p. 13.
11. Fredric Jameson, *The Political Unconscious: Narrative as a socially symbolic act*, Ithaca, N.Y.: Cornell University Press, 1981, p. 44.
12. *Ibid.*, p. 10.
13. See Fredric Jameson, *Postmodernism, or, The Cultural Logic of Late Capitalism*, London and New York: Verso, 1991.
14. Fredric Jameson *Marxism and Form: Twentieth-century dialectical theories of literature*, Princeton, N.J.: Princeton University Press, 1971, p. 163.
15. *Ibid.*, p. 190.
16. *Ibid.*, p. 198.
17. *Ibid.*

Conclusion

1. Bertolt Brecht, 'Against Lukács', translated by Stuart Hood, *New Left Review*, 84 (1974), p. 40.

2. See *RL*, p. 86.
3. Bertolt Brecht, *On Theatre*, translated and edited by J. Willett, London: Eyre & Spottiswode, 1978, p. 204.
4. Charles Jencks, 'Postmodern vs. late-modern', in Ingeborg Hoesterey (ed.), *Zeitgeist in Babel: The post-modern controversy*, Bloomington and Indianapolis, Ind.: Indiana University Press, 1991, pp. 4–21 (p. 4).
5. *Ibid.*, p. 5.
6. *Ibid.*, p. 18.
7. Umberto Eco, *Reflections on the Name of the Rose*, translated by William Weaver, London: Secker & Warburg, 1984, pp. 67–8.
8. Jean-François Lyotard, *The Postmodern Condition: A report on knowledge*, translated by Geoff Bennington and Brian Massumi, Manchester: Manchester University Press, 1984, pp. 37, 60.
9. For a fuller discussion of this topic, see Stuart Sim, *Beyond Aesthetics: Confrontations with poststructuralism and postmodernism*, Hemel Hempstead: Harvester Wheatsheaf, 1992, chapters 7–9.

Select bibliography

Main published works of Georg Lukács

The list below concentrates on Lukács' main books and does not separately record his many articles and essays, which appear in a number of post-Second World War collections. There are numerous editions of Lukács' books, often in several languages, which complicates matters considerably for the bibliographer; the list below gives the first complete edition of each work.

A modern dráma fejlödésének története (*The History of the Development of Modern Drama*), Budapest: Franklin, 1911.

Die Seele und die Formen (*Soul and Form*), Berlin: Fleischel, 1911.

Taktika és etika (*Tactics and Ethics*), Budapest: Kozoktatasi Nepbiztossag Kiadasa, 1919.

Die Theorie des Romans (*The Theory of The Novel*), Berlin: Paul Cassirer, 1920.

Geschichte und Klassenbewusstsein: Studien über Marxistische Dialektik (*History and Class Consciousness*), Berlin: Malik Verlag, 1923.

Lenin: Studie über den Zusammenhang seiner Gedanken (*Lenin: A Study on the Unity of his Thought*), Vienna: Verlag der Arbeiterbuchhandlung, 1924.

A történelmi regény (*The Historical Novel*), Budapest: Hungaria, 1947.

A polgár nyomában: a hetvenéves Thomas Mann (*Essays on Thomas Mann*), Budapest: Hungaria, 1947.

Goethe und seine Zeit (*Goethe and his Age*), Berne: Francke, 1947.

Der Junge Hegel (*The Young Hegel*), Zurich and Vienna: Europa Verlag, 1948.

Existentialisme ou marxisme? (*Existentialism or Marxism?*), Paris: Nagel, 1948.

Essays über Realismus (*Essays on Realism*), Berlin: Aufbau Verlag, 1948.

Karl Marx und Friedrich Engels als Literaturhistoriker (*Karl Marx and Friedrich Engels as Historians of Literature*), Berlin: Aufbau Verlag, 1948.

Der russische Realismus in der Weltliteratur (*Russian Realism in World Literature*), Berlin: Aufbau Verlag, 1949.

Deutsche Realisten des neunzehnten Jahrhunderts (*German Realists of the Nineteenth Century*), Berlin: Aufbau Verlag, 1951.

Studies In European Realism, London: Hillway, 1950.

Balzac und der französische Realismus (*Balzac and French Realism*), Berlin: Aufbau Verlag, 1952.

Die Zerstörung der Vernunft (*The Destruction of Reason*), Berlin: Aufbau Verlag, 1954.

Beiträge zur Geschichte der Aesthetik (*Contributions to the History of Aesthetics*), Berlin: Aufbau Verlag, 1954.

Über die Besonderheit als Kategorie der Aesthetik (*On Specialty as a Category of Aesthetics*), Neuweid: Luchterhand, 1957.

Wider den missverstanden Realismus (*The Meaning of Contemporary Realism*), Hamburg: Claasen, 1958.

Die Eigenart des Aesthetischen (*The Specificity of the Aesthetic*), Neuweid: Luchterhand, 1963.

Writer and Critic and Other Essays, London: Merlin Press, 1970.

Solzhenitsyn, Neuweid and Berlin: Luchterhand, 1969.

Zur ontologie des gesellschaftlichen Seins (*The Ontology of Social Being*), Budapest: Magveto Kiado, 1976.

Record of a Life: an autobiographical sketch (*Gelebtes Denken: eine Autobiographie im Dialog*), Frankfurt-am-Main: Suhrkamp, 1981.

English translations of Georg Lukács

The Destruction of Reason, translated by Peter Palmer, London: Merlin Press, 1980.

Essays on Realism, translated by David Fernbach, edited by Rodney Livingstone, London: Lawrence & Wishart, 1980.

Essays On Thomas Mann, translated by Stanley Mitchell, London: Merlin Press, 1964.

Goethe and his Age, translated by Robert Anchor, London: Merlin Press, 1968.

The Historical Novel, translated by Hannah and Stanley Mitchell, Harmondsworth: Penguin, 1969.

History and Class Consciousness: Studies in Marxist dialectics, translated by Rodney Livingstone, London: Merlin Press, 1971.

Lenin: a study on the unity of his thought, translated by Nicholas Jacobs, London: NLB, 1970.

Marxism and Human Liberation: Essays on history, culture and revolution, edited by E. San Juan Jr, New York: Dell Publishing, 1973.

The Meaning of Contemporary Realism, translated by John and Necke Mander, London: Merlin Press, 1963.

The Ontology of Social Being: 1. Hegel, translated by David Fernbach, London: Merlin Press, 1978.

The Ontology of Social Being: 2. Marx, translated by David Fernbach, London: Merlin Press, 1978.

Political Writings 1919–1929: The question of parliamentarianism and other essays, translated by Michael McColgan, edited by Rodney Livingstone, London: NLB, 1972.

Record of a Life: An autobiographical sketch, translated by Rodney Livingstone, edited by István Eorsi, London: Verso, 1983.

Solzhenitsyn, translated by William David Graf, London: Merlin Press, 1970.

Soul and Form, translated by Anna Bostock, London: Merlin Press, 1974.

Studies in European Realism: A sociological survey of the writings of Balzac, Stendhal, Zola, Tolstoy, Gorki and others, translated by Edith Bone, London: Merlin Press, 1972.

The Theory of the Novel: A historico-philosophical essay on the forms of great epic literature, translated by Anna Bostock, London: Merlin Press, 1971.

Writer and Critic and Other Essays, translated and edited by Arthur Kahn, London: Merlin Press, 1970.

The Young Hegel: Studies in the relations between dialectics and economics, translated by Rodney Livingstone, London: Merlin Press, 1975.

Studies of Georg Lukács

Arato, Andrew and Paul Brienes, *The Young Lukács and the Origins of Western Marxism*, New York: Seabury Press, 1979.

Bernstein, J.M., *The Philosophy of the Novel: Lukács, Marxism, and the dialectics of form*, Minneapolis: University of Minnesota Press, 1984.

Brecht, Bertolt, 'Against Lukács', translated by Stuart Hood, *New Left Review*, 84, (1974), pp. 33–53.

Congdon, Lee, *The Young Lukács*, Chapel Hill, N.C.: University of North Carolina Press, 1983.

Corredor, Eva L., *György Lukács and the Literary Pretext*, New York: Peter Lang, 1987.

de Man, Paul, *Blindness and Insight: Essays in the rhetoric of contemporary criticism*, London: Methuen, 1983.

Demetz, Peter, *Marx, Engels and the Poets*, translated by Jeffrey L. Sammons, Chicago and London: University of Chicago Press, 1967.

Eagleton, Terry, *Marxism and Literary Criticism*, London: Methuen, 1976.

Feenberg, Andrew, *Lukács, Marx and the Sources of Critical Theory*, Oxford: Martin Robertson, 1981.

Gluck, Mary, *Georg Lukács and his Generation, 1900–18*, Cambridge, Mass.: Harvard University Press, 1985.

Goldmann, Lucien, *Lukács and Heidegger: Towards a new philosophy*, translated by William Q. Boelhower, London, Henley, and Boston: Routledge & Kegan Paul, 1977.

Heller, Agnes (ed.), *Lukács Revalued*, Oxford: Basil Blackwell, 1983.

Hyppolite, Jean, *Studies on Marx and Hegel*, translated by John O'Neill, London: Heinemann, 1969.

Jameson, Fredric, *Marxism and Form: Twentieth-century dialectical theories of literature*, Princeton, N.J.: Princeton University Press, 1971.

Jay, Martin, *Marxism and Totality: The adventures of a concept from Lukács to Habermas*, Cambridge and Oxford: Polity Press and Basil Blackwell, 1984.

Joos, Ernest (ed.), *Georg Lukács and his World: A reassessment*, New York: Peter Lang, 1987.

Joos, Ernest, *Lukács' Last Autocriticism*, Atlantic Highlands, N.J.: Humanities Press, 1983.

Kadarkay, Árpád, *Georg Lukács: Life, thought and politics*, Oxford and Cambridge, Mass.: Basil Blackwell, 1991.

Kiralyfalvi, Bela, *The Aesthetics of György Lukács*, Princeton, N.J.: Princeton University Press, 1975.

Lichtheim, George, *Lukács*, London: Fontana/Collins, 1970.

Lowy, Michael, *Georg Lukács – From Romanticism to Bolshevism*, translated by Patrick Camiller, London: NLB, 1979.

Lunn, Eugene, *Marxism and Modernism: An historical study of Lukács, Brecht, Benjamin and Adorno*, Berkeley, Cal.: University of California Press, 1982.

Marcus, Judith, *Georg Lukács and Thomas Mann*, Amherst, Mass.: University of Massachussets Press, 1987.

Marcus, Judith and Zoltán Tarr (eds.), *Georg Lukács: Theory, culture, and politics*, New Brunswick, N.J.: Transaction, 1989.

Mészaros, István, *Lukács' Concept of Dialectic*, London: Merlin Press, 1972.

Parkinson, G. H. R. (ed.), *Georg Lukács: The man, his work and his ideas*, London: Weidenfeld & Nicolson, 1970.

Pinkus, Theo, with Hans Heinz Holz, Leo Kofler and Wolfgang Abendroth, *Conversations with Lukács*, translated by David Fernbach, London: Merlin Press, 1974.

Wellek, René, *Four Critics: Croce, Valéry, Lukács, and Ingarden*, Seattle and London: University of Washington Press, 1981.

Zitta, Victor, *Georg Lukács' Marxism: Alienation, dialectics, revolution. A study in utopia and ideology*, The Hague: Martinus Nijhoff, 1964.

Index

145